A Splash OF ALOHA

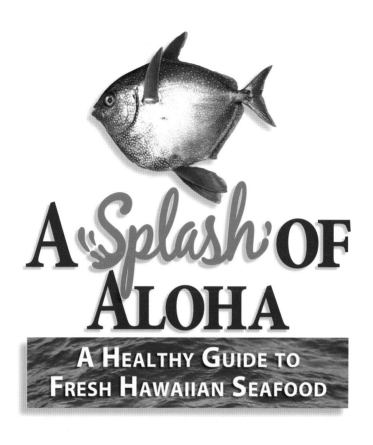

A "Splash" OF ALOHA

A HEALTHY GUIDE TO FRESH HAWAIIAN SEAFOOD

KAPI'OLANI COMMUNITY COLLEGE
University of Hawai'i

WATERMARK
PUBLISHING

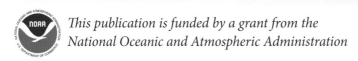

This publication is funded by a grant from the National Oceanic and Atmospheric Administration

Principal Investigator: Ron Takahashi, Chair, MBA, CHE, CFBE, Culinary Arts Department, Kapiʻolani Community College, University of Hawaiʻi

Co-Investigator: Dr. Corilee Watters, Assistant Professor, Department of Human Nutrition, Food and Animal Science, University of Hawaiʻi

Special thanks to the following organizations and individuals for their contributions:

- *Dr. John Kaneko, Hawaiʻi Seafood Council—mercury-selenium interaction and omega-3 fatty acid content data, pelagic fish and Hawaiʻi fishery photos*
- *Dr. Corilee Watters and students of the Department of Human Nutrition, Food and Animal Science, University of Hawaiʻi (Scott Iwamura and Lee Rosner)—nutrition analysis and research data*
- *National Oceanic and Atmospheric Administration—fish illustrations*
- *Hawaiʻi State Department of Agriculture*

  Hawaiʻi aquaculture product photos
- *United Fishing Agency, Honolulu Fish Auction and Brooks Takenaka*
- *Natural Energy Laboratory of Hawaiʻi Authority*
- *American Heart Association*
- *Whole Foods Market, Kāhala*
- *Hawaiʻi's fishermen and fisherwomen and the Hawaiʻi seafood industry*

ISBN: 978-1-935690-13-9

Library of Congress Control Number:
2012938544

Culinary photography
Adriana Torres Chong

Design and production
Gonzalez Design

Watermark Publishing
1088 Bishop Street, Suite 310, Honolulu, Hawaiʻi 96813
Telephone 1-808-587-7766
Toll-free 1-866-900-BOOK
sales@bookshawaii.net
www.bookshawaii.net

Printed in China

Contents

Foreword

by Wanda A. Adams
Food editor, writer and blogger

After spending my childhood as a country girl on Maui, and the last 22 years as a food writer on Oʻahu, after writing three cookbooks and editing another, after dozens of interviews with old-timers, hours and hours in the library of the *Honolulu Advertiser* and various local book repositories, after collecting 25 linear feet of community cookbooks—well, after all that, you'd think I knew something about every possible subject related to Island food.

You'd be wrong. I didn't know anything about Hawaiʻi fish. I grew up in the mountains and none of my family were fishermen. The only fish my grandmother put on the table was canned (tuna and sardines) or dried (bacalhau, salt cod). My mother hates fish and never served it. Having lived in the Pacific Northwest for 20 years mid-career, I knew way more about salmon and halibut than I did about shutome and ulua. I could more readily name the types of clams and mussels than I could tell an ʻopihi from a pipipi. I knew just enough to know that fish is a complicated and controversial topic. And I was actively afraid of cooking it.

I rarely prepare fish at home, though I always feel as though I should. But get me much beyond mahimahi and monchong and I'm lost. The last time I went on an eat-more-fish crusade, I brought home something that was so bony and so disgustingly fishy flavored that I almost cried. I've learned to make a few fish dishes well: furikake salmon, a Venetian shrimp appetizer, monchong in a fresh tomato sauce, grilled ʻahi with a thickened teri drizzle.

So editing this book was like being thrown into a doctoral course from kindergarten. My computer spent so much time at the informative site operated by the Hawaiʻi Seafood Council (www.Hawaii-seafood.org) that I might as well have made it my home page. From my stash of community cookbooks, I dug out *The Fishes of the Pacific from the Fishwife* (1986) by Shirley Rizzuto, a longtime columnist for the *Hawaiʻi Fishing News; How to Hook and Cookbook* (1988) by TV personality Mike Sakamoto; and chef Elmer Guzman's more recent *The Shoreline Chef: Creative Cuisine for Hawaiian Reef Fish* (2003). Big thanks to those folks.

Like every newbie, I struggled with fish nomenclature: An aʻu is a nairagi is a striped marlin, but so is a kajiki (blue marlin) because aʻu is the generic Hawaiian name for all marlins. Japanese names, Hawaiian names, English names, casual names and formal names, incorrect names. The fish world is the land of "call it what you will, just call me in time for dinner."

The species represented here are among the best known in Island waters, but the list is hardly comprehensive. Besides learning the names and attributes of the more than 20 varieties of seafood we chose to profile, the chefs and teachers who contributed these nearly 100 recipes taught me techniques for bringing out the best in fish of different types: what to grill and what to braise, what to make into soup and what to eat raw.

The biggest compliment I can give any cookbook is that reading it made me want to put my apron on and get into the kitchen. The recipes here did that time and again. There will be a lot more fish on our table in the future—and a lot less trepidation on the part of the cook.

Inside the Honolulu Fish Auction at Pier 38

Introduction
Somewhere beyond the Sea...

by Daniel Leung, MSW, AS (Culinary Arts)
Kapiʻolani Community College

F rom the depths of the clear, blue Hawaiian sea comes a bounty of seafood that has played a prominent role in bringing Hawaii's regional cuisine to worldwide fame. While these ingredients from the deep—pelagic fish living in open waters such as

- tombo (albacore)
- ʻahi (yellow fin tuna)
- aku (skipjack tuna)
- kajiki (blue marlin)
- nairagi (striped marlin or aʻu)
- hebi (shortbill spearfish)
- shutome (broadbill swordfish)
- opah (moonfish)
- ono (wahoo)

are commonly offered in restaurants—not all home cooks are familiar with them or know the best ways to prepare them. Yet these fish are a healthy and safe source of protein because they live in clean, unpolluted waters throughout the Hawaiian island chain. Living in deep, cold water they also develop a high-quality fat content that not only keeps their flesh moist for cooking but also makes them a great source of beneficial omega-3 fatty acids.

The chart on page 4 on selenium levels in Hawaiʻi seafood shows that consumers need not worry about significant mercury in their seafood. While concerns have been raised about the mercury level in seafood, this consideration alone does not present the whole picture on seafood safety. Smart consumers should also take into account the level of selenium in a fish, as selenium interacts or binds with mercury, reducing its harmful effect.

A Hawaiʻi seafood cookbook is not complete without including some of the traditional favorites—mahimahi (dolphinfish), monchong (sickle pomfret), hāpuʻupuʻu (Hawaiian grouper) and popular bottom fish such as ʻopakapaka (pink snapper), onaga (red snapper) and uku (grey snapper). Yet several of these popular fish have been threatened in recent years by overfishing, leading to a scarcity in the grocery stores and pushing prices to all-time highs. To allow the fish stocks to regenerate, a periodic fishing moratorium is imposed by the Western Pacific Fishery Management Council and territorial, commonwealth or state authorities that jointly manage the Western Pacific bottom fish fisheries (an area that geographically encompasses the main Hawaiian Islands, the Northwestern Hawaiian Islands, Guam, the Commonwealth of the Northern Mariana Islands and American Samoa). As the ancient Hawaiians knew well, there is a season for everything. So, if you're looking for wonderful fish to enjoy, especially when budget is an issue, it is very useful to have tasty recipes that incorporate the wide range of fresh fish and other fresh, locally raised seafood (such as prawns, abalone, tilapia) that is available. So, think of it this way: By including more locally caught open-ocean fish in your diet, you're not only eating healthier, you're also helping to ensure the viability of a major food source. There is a fish for every occasion!

Another growing concern related to seafood is the rapid rise in the worldwide demand for seafood. The ocean can no longer sustain the rate of consumption. One emerging solution is aquaculture—"farming" seafood on land or just offshore. Hawaiʻi is among the world leaders in this new industry, raising seafood with cold, nutrient-rich, pathogen-free seawater pumped up from 2,000 feet deep off Keāhole Point on the Big Island of Hawaiʻi, at the ocean science and technology park managed by the Natural Energy Laboratory of Hawaiʻi Authority. Hawaiʻi-grown abalone, butterfish (black cod) and kampachi (amberjack) are among the commercial successes thus far. On the other Hawaiian islands are fish and shrimp farms producing moi (Pacific threadfin), tilapia, mullet, prawns and shrimp. These homegrown products are clean tasting and healthy, as a result of careful management of their feed and water environment. And, they are becoming more commonly available on a regular basis—clean, fresh, healthy and ready for your dinner table.

A Splash of Aloha is a cookbook that introduces these sources of quality seafood to those who are looking for simple, quick ways to cook a delicious dinner for the family, as well as those who would like to venture into new culinary territories. Recipe contributors are from among the faculty and chef instructors of the Culinary Institute of the Pacific at Kapiʻolani Community College (KCC), with "guest appearances" from well-known Hawaiʻi Regional Cuisine chefs, chef instructors from the popular continuing education program at KCC and editor and food writer Wanda Adams. The cooking methods described in these pages are wide ranging, producing a myriad of flavors from Hawaiʻi and Asia to the Middle East, Mexico and Italy, and every one is designed with the home cook in mind.

So bon appétit, as you gaze towards the horizon and beyond the sea— as somewhere, a plate of delicious, healthy Hawaiʻi seafood is waiting for you.

Part I

A Guide to Hawaiian Seafood

Healthy Seafood Hawaii

Long-Chain Omega-3s (EPA and DHA) and Selenium

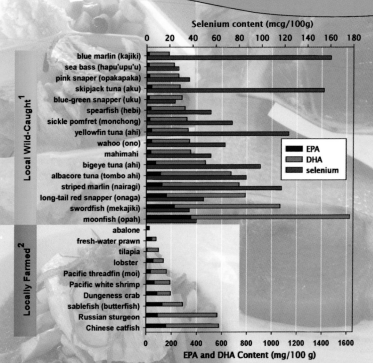

Selenium content (mcg/100g)

0 20 40 60 80 100 120 140 160 180

Local Wild-Caught[1]

- blue marlin (kajiki)
- sea bass (hapu'upu'u)
- pink snaper (opakapaka)
- skipjack tuna (aku)
- blue-green snapper (uku)
- spearfish (hebi)
- sickle pomfret (monchong)
- yellowfin tuna (ahi)
- wahoo (ono)
- mahimahi
- bigeye tuna (ahi)
- albacore tuna (tombo ahi)
- striped marlin (nairagi)
- long-tail red snapper (onaga)
- swordfish (mekajiki)
- moonfish (opah)

Locally Farmed[2]

- abalone
- fresh-water prawn
- tilapia
- lobster
- Pacific threadfin (moi)
- Pacific white shrimp
- Dungeness crab
- sablefish (butterfish)
- Russian sturgeon
- Chinese catfish

EPA
DHA
selenium

0 200 400 600 800 1000 1200 1400 1600

EPA and DHA Content (mg/100 g)

Dietetic Associations recommend consuming two 3.5 ounce (~100g) servings of fatty fish per week, or an average of 500 mg of *Eicosapentaenoic acid* (EPA) and *Docosahexaenoic acid* (DHA) daily.

[1]Data for local wild-caught fish species provided by Hawaii Seafood Council. Wild Hawaii Fish. Retrieved from http://www.hawaii-seafood.org.

[2]Locally Farmed EPA and DHA data (selenium levels not tested) provided by Watters, C., Rosner, L, Franke A. 2011. Retrieved from http://www2.hawaii.edu/~cwatters/healthyseafoodhawaii.html.

* Selenium may be protective against methylmercury exposure.

HawaiiSeafood
Hawaii Seafood Council

UNIVERSITY of HAWAI'I
MĀNOA

CHAPTER ONE

Healthy Seafood, Hawaiian Style

by Karl Sloss and Dr. Corilee Watters
*University of Hawaiʻi College of Tropical Agriculture
and Human Resources*

Seafood is an important part of a healthy diet. Fish are low in saturated fat and are an excellent source of protein. Seafood is not only a good source of numerous vitamins and minerals including vitamin D, vitamin B_{12}, iron, calcium, iodine and selenium but is also one of the few dietary sources of the omega-3 fatty acids EPA (eicosapentaenoic acid) and DHA (docosahexaenoic acid). You can obtain other forms of omega-3 fatty acids, such as ALA (α-linolenic acid), from plant-based foods, but these forms are not associated with the numerous health benefits you can obtain by eating seafood rich in

Omega-3-rich Hawaiian pelagic fish fillet

EPA and DHA. Both the American Dietetic Association and the Dietitians of Canada recommend consuming two portions (about 4 ounces each) of fatty fish per week to obtain about 500 mg of EPA and DHA per day[1].

Beneficial Effects of Omega-3s in Adults

Omega-3 fatty acids have been receiving a lot of attention in recent years for their role in maintaining heart health. The FDA has approved the health claim that omega-3 fatty acids can lower the risk of cardiovascular disease. Although this claim can be found on products containing plant-based omega-3s as well as fish sources, scientific trials have shown that it is primarily EPA and DHA fatty acids, such as those found in fish, that protect the heart[2]. The benefits of omega-3s in seafood are not limited to reduced risk of cardiovascular disease, however. EPA and DHA have also been shown to reduce inflammation and improve the health of those suffering from certain arthritic conditions and also may play a role in the prevention of cancer, may help you maintain mental function during aging and can reduce the symptoms of asthma in some children[3]. Omega-3 fatty acids from seafood have also been shown to maintain eye health through aging and reduce the incidence of age-related macular degeneration[4].

Beneficial Effects of Omega 3's in Childhood Development

Omega-3 fatty acids in seafood also play an important role in healthy childhood development. EPA and DHA have been shown to support nerve development and brain function[5]. DHA in particular is a large component of grey matter in the human brain. Studies have found that consumption of EPA and DHA by infants through breast milk or formula is associated with improved eyesight and higher intelligence[3,5].

Mercury and PCB Contaminant Concerns

Many individuals are concerned about the safety of seafood due to environmental contaminants. One of the contaminants of greatest concern, especially for pregnant women, nursing mothers and young children, is methylmercury. The Hawai'i State Department of Health publishes a guide on safe fish consumption for this segment of the population. The guide lists a few fish species that should be avoided (kajiki, shark, swordfish) and several more that should be limited ('ahi, ono, opah, aku, grouper, mahimahi, nairagi) but stresses that fish consumption is part of a healthy diet. If you are not in this segment of the population, there is no evidence that fish consumption needs to be limited due to methylmercury concerns. Hawai'i seafood tends to have a high level of selenium compared to fish from other areas, and selenium is

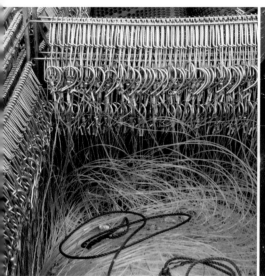

thought to protect against the effects of methylmercury[6].

Another group of contaminants often associated with seafood is polychlorinated biphenyls or PCBs. Levels of PCBs in ocean fish, however, have been found to be comparable to beef, chicken or cheese, although levels in farm-raised fish may be higher[7]. Numerous experts have examined all of the data and concluded that the health benefits of consuming seafood outweigh the risks[8].

Freshness and Quality

Another advantage of consuming local seafood in Hawai'i is its freshness and quality. The Honolulu Fish Auction, held at Pier 38 at Honolulu Harbor, is modeled after the Tokyo fish auction and is open to the public. This model allows fishermen to get higher prices for high-quality fish and at the same time offers wholesale pricing to seafood processors and restaurants. The Honolulu Fish Auction is the source for much of the local seafood sold in restaurants and grocery stores in the state. All fish are hook-and-line caught, and the fishery has met the requirements of the Food and Agriculture Organization of the United Nations to be labeled as sustainable. Fish sold at the auction vary with availability but include 'ahi (bigeye, yellowfin), tombo 'ahi (albacore), aku (skipjack tuna), kajiki (blue marlin), nairagi (striped marlin), hebi (shortbill spearfish), mekajiki, mahimahi, ono (wahoo), opah (moonfish), monchong (sickle pomfret), onaga (long-tail red snapper), 'opakapaka (pink snapper), uku (blue-green snapper) and hāpu'upu'u (grouper or sea bass).

Aquaculture

Another important factor in Island seafood is the local aquaculture industry. Aquaculture can control the nutritional value (such as the level of fatty acids) and taste of fish and other seafood products through their diet (feed). Currently, Hawai'i is one of the leaders in research and development in the industry. At the forefront is the National Energy Laboratory of Hawai'i Authority (NELHA) located at Keāhole Point on the Kona Coast of the Big Island. At NELHA cold, nutrient-rich deep ocean water from below 2,000 feet is pumped to the surface and used for growing different species of fish and shellfish. This deep sea water is currently used for the mariculture of Maine lobster, dungeness crab, moi (Pacific threadfin), hirame, abalone, sablefish (butterfish), kampachi and various types of seaweed such as ogo and dulse. In addition, the University of Hawai'i has devoted significant resources to the development of freshwater aquaculture systems on other islands as well, producing high-quality products such as tilapia (sunfish), mullet, catfish, prawns and limu (seaweed).

Opposite page: Fishing boat lines and a fresh-caught uku at the Honolulu Fish Auction. Left and above: Prawns and abalone are among the many products raised in Hawai'i's aquaculture industry.

Live Hawaiian farm-raised tilapia on sale in markets in Honolulu's Chinatown

References

(1) Kris-Etherton, P, Grieger, J, Etherton, TD. 2009. Dietary Reference Intakes for DHA and EPA. *Prostaglandins, Leukotrienes, and Essential Fatty Acids* 81(2-3): 99-104.

(2) Kris-Etherton PM, Harris WS, Appel LJ. 2003. Fish Consumption, fish oil, omega 3 fatty acids and cardiovascular disease. *Arteriosclerosis, Thrombosis and Vascular Biology* 23: e20-e30.

(3) Horrocks LA, Yeo YK. 1999. Health benefits of Docosaheaenoic Acid (DHA). *Pharmacologic Research* 40 (3): 211-225.

(4) Zhang C, Bazan NG. 2010. Lipid-mediated cell signaling protects against injury and neurodegeneration. *Journal of Nutrition* 140 (4): 858-63.

(5) Neuringer M, Anderson GJ, Connor WE. 1988. The essentiality of n-3 fatty acids for the development and function of the retina and brain. *Annual Review Nutrition* 8: 517-41.

(6) Kaneko, J.J., Ralston, N.V. 2007. Selenium and mercury in pelagic fish in the central north Pacific near Hawaiʻi. *Biol Trace Elem Res* 119(3):242-54.

(7) Schecter A, Cramer P, Boggess K, Stanley J, Päpke O, Olson J, Silver A, Schmitz M. 2001. Intake of dioxins and related compounds from food in the U.S. population. *J Toxicol Env Heal*, part A, 63:1–18.

(8) Mozaffarian D, Rimm EB. 2006. Fish intake, contaminants, and human health: evaluating the risks and the benefits. *JAMA* 296(15):1885-1899.

CHAPTER TWO

2

The Heart-Healthy Benefits of Eating Fish

by Dr. Stephen Bradley
The American Heart Association

Fish is a fine source of protein and, unlike meat products, is not high in saturated fat. Fish is also a good source of omega-3 fatty acids, which benefit the hearts of healthy people, and those at high risk of or who have cardiovascular disease. Research has shown that omega-3 fatty acids decrease risk of arrhythmias (abnormal heartbeats), which can lead to sudden death. Omega-3 fatty acids also decrease triglyceride levels, slow growth rate of atherosclerotic plaque and lower blood pressure (slightly). Recent research has indicated the other kinds of omega acids, called long-chain acids, found in fish are even more beneficial (see Chapter 1).

The American Heart Association (AHA) recommends eating fish, particularly fatty fish, at least twice a week. Each serving should be about 3.5 ounces cooked, or about 3/4 cup flaked fish. Fatty fish such as salmon, mackerel, herring, trout, sardines and tuna are high in omega-3 fatty acids.

It has been shown that increasing omega-3 fatty acid consumption through foods is preferable to the use of supplements, although these still have a place in increasing the available levels in the body.

How Omega-3 Fatty Acids May Reduce the Risk of Cardiovascular Disease

- Reducing susceptibility of the heart to irregular rhythms
- Reducing the tendency of the blood to clot
- Lowering triglycerides (fasting and postprandial)
- Retarding growth of atherosclerotic plaque
- Reducing platelet-derived growth factor
- Anti-inflammatory characteristics
- Promoting nitric oxide-induced endothelial relaxation of the blood vessels
- Mild effect in promoting lower blood pressure

Omega-3 fatty acids have been shown in epidemiological and clinical trials to reduce the incidence of cardiovascular disease. Large-scale epidemiological studies suggest that individuals at risk for coronary heart disease benefit from the consumption of plant- and marine-derived omega-3 fatty acids, although we are not yet sure just how much fish would produce the best effects. Evidence from prospective secondary prevention studies suggests that supplementing your diet with 0.5 to 1.8 grams per day of the essential fatty acids EPA (eicosapentanaenoic acid) and DHA (docosahexaenoic acid), either as fatty fish or supplements, significantly reduces cardiac and other forms of death.

Collectively, these data are supportive of the recommendation made by the AHA Dietary Guidelines to include at least two servings of fish per week (particularly fatty fish).

In synthesis, fish consumption has been found beneficial in all of the following areas:

Heart Health

Doctors have known of strong links between fish and healthy hearts ever since they noticed that fish-eating Inuit populations in the Arctic had low levels of heart disease. One study has suggested that adding one portion of fish a week to your diet can cut your chances of suffering a heart attack by half.

Fish is thought to protect the heart because eating less saturated fat and more omega-3s can help to lower the amount of cholesterol and triglycerides in the blood—two fats that, in excess, increase the risk of heart disease. Omega-3 fats also have natural built-in anti-oxidants, which are thought to stop the thickening and damaging of artery walls.

Regularly eating fish oils is also thought to reduce the risk of arrhythmia—irregular electrical activity in the heart, which increases the risk of sudden heart attacks.

Brain Functionality

The human brain is 10- to 12-percent lipids, including the omega-3 fat DHA. Recent studies suggest that older people can boost their brain power by eating more oily fish, and those who enjoy such fish regularly, are able to remember better and think faster than those who eat none. Other research has also suggested that adding more DHA to the diet of children with attention-deficit hyperactivity disorder can reduce their behavioral problems and improve their reading skills, while there have also been links suggested between DHA and better concentration. Separate studies have suggested that older people who eat fish at least once a week could also have a lower chance of developing Alzheimer's disease and other types of dementia.

Depression

Published studies have suggested benefits in increasing fish consumption for patients suffering from depression and other psychological ailments.

Asthma

The anti-inflammatory properties of omega-3 fatty acids have been shown to be beneficial to patients suffering from asthma. Children who eat fish may be less likely to develop asthma. Asthma is a significant problem among Hawai'i's children.

Diabetes

Studies have shown that fish consumption helps patients control their blood sugar and also appears to improve kidney function; renal deterioration is one of the hallmarks of advancing Type II diabetes.

Joint Benefits

Including fish as a regular part of a balanced diet has been shown to ameliorate the symptoms of rheumatoid arthritis, a painful and often debilitating condition that causes joints to swell up, reducing strength and mobility. Studies also show that sufferers feel less stiff and sore in the morning if they keep their fish oil intake topped up.

Recent research has also found a link between omega-3 fats and a slowing down in the wearing of cartilage that leads to osteoarthritis, opening the door for more research into whether eating more fish could help prevent the disease.

Possible Benefits against Macular Degeneration

Some studies have shown regular fish consumption to be highly protective against this blindness-causing disease in older persons.

Iodine, Selenium, Vitamin A and Zinc

Fish is high in minerals such as iodine and selenium, which keep the body running smoothly. Iodine is essential for the thyroid gland, which controls growth and metabolism, while selenium is used to make enzymes that protect cell walls from cancer-causing free radicals and helps prevent DNA damage caused by radiation and some chemicals.

Fish is also an excellent source of vitamin A, which is needed for healthy skin and eyes, and vitamin D, which is needed to help the body absorb calcium to strengthen teeth and bones.

Yellowfin tuna displayed at the Honolulu Fish Auction

CHAPTER THREE

Hawai'i Seafood Safety: Keeping the Best at Its Best

by Henry Holthaus, CEC
Chief-Instructor, Kapi'olani Community College

Hawai'i's people have access to some of the freshest—and therefore the safest and most flavorful—seafood on the planet. The Island fishing fleet harvests wild fish from 900-1,500 miles around the state, while our aquaculture industry "farms" the near waters.

There are two different definitions of freshness:

• *Fresh* means a food that has never been frozen or preserved in any other way. Keeping fresh fish safe and in top condition means shortening the time between harvest and consumption and keeping the fish or shellfish very, very cold—packed in ice aboard ship, chilled and properly protected on land.

• *Fresh* also means having the least amount of time from the ocean to the consumer, while being kept cold (chilled at a temperature of less than or equal to 41°F).

The critical factors for eating healthy and safe seafood in Hawai'i are:

• Hazards associated with the fish and its source
• Time to table and temperature control during that time
• Personal hygiene of food handlers
• Cross-contamination (when one food contaminates another food through contact with a common surface or by dripping)

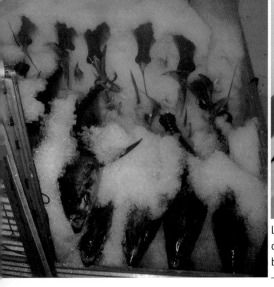

Left: Packing fish in ice aboard ship is vital to the safety of Island seafood. Above: Fresh whole fish should have bright red gills.

Fresh whole fish should have bulging eyes.

Whole fish that aren't fresh have red-rimmed or sunken eyes.

Wet and Wild-Caught

What are some of the hazards associated with Hawai'i's wild catch? If the fish you buy came through the United Fishing Agency, the state's daily fish auction, be assured that it was handled properly in the immense, frigid warehouse on Pier 38. If there's a problem with fish that passed through the auction, the mishandling is most likely the fault of the distributor, the retail store from which you bought it or your own handling. Also, fish caught and sold privately—even by a professional fisherman—comes with no guarantees.

To assure that you're buying really fresh wild-caught fish, follow these guidelines:

- Fresh fish don't smell like ammonia or overly fishy. Rather, they should smell like a fresh ocean breeze.
- Fresh whole fish should have bulging eyes and bright red gills; don't buy fish with eyes that are deeply sunken or red-rimmed.
- The same standards apply when you buy fish from a private source.

Issues of Concern

Ciguatera This is a food-borne intoxication contracted from tropical and subtropical predator reef fish. The culprit is the *Gambierdiscus toxicus*, a dinoflagellate, which works its way up the food chain to the larger fish. All predator tropical reef fish such as groupers, barracudas, snappers, jacks, mackerels and triggerfish should be suspect but are not necessarily toxic. Ciguatera cannot be detected by sight, smell or taste and cannot be cooked out of the fish. In addition to causing vomiting and diarrhea the toxin can, among other disorders, affect the nervous system, causing tingling sensations and a reversal of hot and cold sensations. Your best protection is to buy from a reputable supplier or test the fish yourself. Test kits are available at fishing supply stores or online for those who want to test the fish that they buy or catch.

Scombroid poisoning This type of food-borne intoxication occurs from eating fish such as tuna, ono, mahimahi or marlin that has not been properly handled. Letting the fish get too warm results in the formation of toxic histamines by bacteria in the fish. Histamines are not destroyed by freezing, cooking, smoking, drying, jerking or curing. The symptoms may include reddening of the face or neck, headache, sweating or a burning/tingling sensation in the mouth or throat, with the possibility of vomiting and diarrhea to follow. To protect yourself, deal only with a reputable fish supplier such as the United Fishing Agency. The goal of any reputable fish handler is to keep the core temperature of the fish at 36-40°F (2-4°C).

Anisakis This illness is caused by ingesting the live anisakis parasite present in certain species of undercooked or raw fish. It can cause stomach pain, nausea, vomiting, sometimes anaphylaxis (a severe allergic reaction) and the most alarming symptom—coughing up worms! The most common fish to carry the parasite include herring, cod, mackerel and Pacific salmon. Herring (akule) and mackerel (ono) can be found in Hawaiian waters. Be sure not to eat these unless they're fully cooked and well done to an internal temperature of 145°F (63°C), which kills the parasite. Freezing to a core temperature of -4°F (-20°C) or below for 24 hours or more will also kill this parasite. This doesn't mean that these fish always carry anisakis, but use safe practices. Tuna and billfish, which we eat as sashimi and poke, do not carry the anisakis parasite.

Mercury This has been a hot-button issue and must be considered a safety concern. According to John Kaneko, a researcher for the Hawai'i Seafood Council, it's not just a question of how much mercury is in a fish but of the ratio of mercury to selenium. Mercury inhibits the body's use of selenium, a trace mineral essential to good health. If there is more selenium than mercury in fish, there is less risk of illness. However, pregnant women should follow different guidelines, which can be found in the Environmental Protection Agency mercury guidelines (http://water.epa.gov/scitech/swguidance/fishshellfish/outreach/advice_index.cfm).

Hawai'i fish studied by Kaneko and his team included striped marlin, yellowfin tuna, mahimahi, skipjack tuna, spearfish, ono, monchong, albacore tuna, big-eye tuna, blue marlin, opah, thresher shark, swordfish, akule, pink and blue-green snapper and Hawaiʻi sea bass. All but one of these had a favorable Selenium Health Benefit Value (SeHBV). The only fish studied that did not have a favorable SeHBV was mako shark. See: http://www.Hawaii-sea-food.org/uploads/2010%20Symposium/Kaneko-John%20Abstract.pdf.

Seafood Raised in Hawaiʻi

What about aquaculture? Among the fish and shellfish that are being or have been raised in Island waters, lakes, reservoirs or tanks are black cod (sablefish), moi, prawns, tilapia, abalone, lobster, crab and kampachi (jack fish). With aquaculture, the greatest concerns are whether or not the feed is safe, the growing environment is clean and the fish are fresh and cold.

Aquaculture operations in Hawaiʻi are regulated by the State Depart-ment of Agriculture, which monitors health hazards in the growing process, including the quality of the water, the feed and the harvesting process. To date, there have been no outbreaks of scombroid, ciguatera or anisakis attrib-uted to Hawaiʻi's aquaculture industry.

In the case of the black cod, lobster, crab and abalone grown on the Big Island at the Natural Energy Laboratory of Hawaiʻi, the water is pumped up from 2,000-3,000 feet deep in the ocean off the Kona-Kohala Coast. This water is extremely clean and delivered on shore at 43°F (6°C). The frigid water mimics northern waters where these fish grow wild. The low temperature also encourages development of beneficial fatty acids.

Another positive feature of Hawaiʻi aquaculture is that in most cases growers harvest on demand, so the seafood remains in the water until orders are received.

Shopping and Storing

What are the issues to consider when you're shopping for fish and transporting it home? For starters, buy it cold and buy it fresh. The safest seafood to buy should be sitting in a bed of ice, or kept chilled below 41°F, in a covered display case. When buying whole fish, examine the body. Any fish that shows signs of puncture (speared or damaged) is exposed to bacterial infection internally.

Also, carbon monoxide and "tasteless smoke" is a controversial but little understood issue. Some seafood processors use either carbon monoxide (CO, a bland, odorless gas) or tasteless smoke (created at a temperature lower than 850°F and then filtered to remove any taste or smell) to preserve and enhance the color in fish that is to be frozen, and to give it a bright cherry-red color that holds up after thawing. Since the color of fresh tuna is the dominant feature in determining quality, grade and price, this presents an opportunity for unscrupulous processors to trick the consumer by using this method to hide the effects of old or lower-quality tuna. The U.S. Food and Drug Administration (FDA) requires that all CO or tasteless smoke-treated fish be labeled as such. The best way to protect yourself is to buy fresh Hawai'i-caught tuna, which is generally never treated in this way. If you're not sure where the fish is from, ask the seller, who is required to answer you truthfully. The point should be made that CO-treated fish is safe to eat if it has been processed properly. You should, however, be skeptical about fish, sashimi or poke that looks too good to be true.

Packing seafood sandwiched with ice packs inside a cooler is a good way to transport it home from the market.

Carry a cooler in your car, with ice or frozen gel-ice packs to keep the fish cold as you drive home. Buy fish last on a shopping trip. Some stores now offer complimentary gel-packs with fish you purchase, or a bag of ice if you ask. At the very least, keep the fish under something frozen, such as ice cream.

Prevent cross-contamination by not storing packaged or wrapped fish above or next to any ready-to-eat food, food to be eaten raw or household cleansers, and not below any meats. Once you've purchased fish, go straight home.

At home, put the fish in the refrigerator first. Note that most home refrigerators cannot adequately avoid cross-contamination (dripping fish juices touching other food). For example, produce drawers are usually on the bottom, although they should be on top so that no blood or fish juice can drip into them. So where in the refrigerator should you store your fish? Put it somewhere where it won't drip on anything, or in an airtight plastic container with a lid in the coldest part of the refrigerator, and use it as soon as possible.

If you only use part of a large cut of fresh fish, wrap the unused portion tightly in plastic wrap or seal lock bags. Label it with a date and put it in the refrigerator. It will still be good for cooking for two more days.

Cooking Fish

Wash your hands before and after touching food. Be sure to clean and sanitize the utensils, cutting board and counter before and after preparing the fish. To make a sanitizing solution, mix one tablespoon of bleach in a gallon of water and soak or wipe everything down. Allow to air-dry.

Another unpleasant subject: Don't use your fingers to taste. Don't double-dip spoons or other utensils and don't allow your saliva or bodily fluids to contaminate the fish. Wash your hands thoroughly with soap and hot water before touching or tasting. The safest way is to use a spoon for tasting and wash and rinse the spoon between tastings.

To serve fish safely: If the fish is raw (sashimi, poke or a tartare-style preparation) and has been sitting in the Temperature Danger Zone (TDZ), it should be eaten within four hours. The TDZ is the temperature range at which bacteria grows best, 41-135°F or 5-57°C. The middle of the TDZ, 70-110°F or 21-43°C, is where bacteria grow the fastest and is also the temperature range of most homes in Hawai'i. You can minimize the hazard by placing the bowl or plate of fish on ice or serving small portions and refreshing from the refrigerator. Raw fish leftovers should be cooked the next day, not served raw again, even if refrigerated.

The TDZ rule also applies to cooked fish. The FDA recommends cooking fish to a minimum internal temperature of 145°F (63°C), meaning well-done, no pink. However, many of us who love seafood would never do this to a good piece of fish. The safest way to break this rule is to use very fresh fish that's been kept cold throughout handling and is being eaten as soon as possible. Once it is cooked, hold fish hot at 135°F (57°C) or higher. Leftovers should not be allowed to sit but should be cooled to 41°F (5°C) within four hours. Fish cools rapidly in the refrigerator if you place a sealed bag of ice on top of the wrapped or covered fish. If you have handled it properly, you can eat fish cold or reheat it to 165°F (74°C). Leftover blackened or seared fish likewise should be kept cold and reheated thoroughly the next day.

How long can you hold fresh or leftover fish? Despite the FDA's Model Food Code standard, which holds that food is safe to eat for seven days after it's been cooked, one or two days at the most is a much better guarantee of safety. (After all, what if you don't remember how long that fish has been in the refrigerator?) A good rule of thumb: When in doubt, throw it out!

Buy it fresh, keep it cold and prepare it and eat it as soon as possible.

CHAPTER FOUR

Fish Preparation and Cooking Methods

H ere are a few cooking procedures that are best suited for fresh Island fish. Simplicity is the key to retaining the true taste and texture of the fish. A few tips before you start:

1. Make sure you wash your hands thoroughly.

2. When cooking whole fish, rinse the fish in cold water first, then blot it dry with a paper towel.

3. For fish fillets, blot dry with a paper towel before cooking. Keep your work surface dry also.

4. Always make sure the sauté pan is hot before adding oil and then the fish. If the fish sticks, that means your pan wasn't hot enough when you put the fish in.

5. Don't leave the fish in the pan after it is done. Serve the fish as soon as it is cooked to your desired doneness. Fish will continue to cook even after it is removed from the pan.

How to Sauté a Fillet (with a Light Dusting of Flour)

1. This method is best for fish with firm texture—any open-ocean fish with high fat content such as opah, shutome, hebi or nairagi.

2. Assemble a simple set-up of oil, pepper and salt (Hawaiian or sea salt).

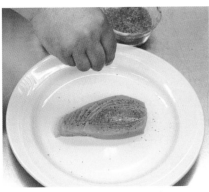

3. Season the fish on both sides with salt and pepper.

4. Dusting: Dredge the fillet in flour; shake off excess flour to leave just a thin layer on both sides.

5. Heat a sauté pan at medium-high heat. When the pan is hot, add a small amount of oil (about 1 tablespoon).

6. Place the fillet in the pan to sauté, presentation side down.

7. Check, and turn over when it is golden brown.

8. Cook the other side until it is also golden brown, or to desired doneness.

9. Place on serving plate and garnish or add your favorite sauce.

Filleting a Whole Fish

1. Best for a whole fresh fish. Buy the fish scaled and cleaned. Rinse it under cold water and blot dry.

2. With a sharp boning knife, make your first cut from the bottom upwards around the side of the collar and stop at the top.

3. Make second cut on the back of the fish starting from behind the head.

4. Cut along the back towards the tail, moving the knife against the bones.

5. Cut all the way to the tail.

6. Repeat from the tail end of the belly of the fish.

7. Cut all the way along the belly towards the head.

8. Insert the knife into the first cut made around the collar.

9. Push and flatten the knife along the backbone, using the two cuts along the back and belly as guides.

10. Slice horizontally, towards the tail end, with the knife pressed flat against the backbone all the way.

11. Cut until the knife exits through the tail end.

12. Lift the fillet off the fish.

13. Fish with fillet removed. Note there is no flesh remaining attached to the bone.

14. Remove the rib bones by cutting from the backbone above the belly.

15. Cut out the rib bones along with the flesh attached.

16. Remove and discard the rib bones.

17. Run your index finger along the belly to feel for pin bones (tip of bones stuck to the flesh).

18. Remove pin bones with tweezers. The fillet is now ready to sauté with skin on.

Removing Skin from a Fish Fillet

1. Make a small incision into the flesh at the tail end until the knife reaches the skin, but do not cut through the skin.

2. Wedge the knife between the skin and flesh and slide forward, while holding the skin with your other hand.

3. Continue the cut along the length of the fillet towards the head end.

4. Finish the cut with your knife exiting the other end of the fillet.

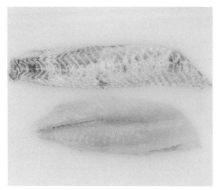

5. Remove the skin from the flesh. The fillet is now ready for use.

How to Sauté a Fish Fillet with the Skin On

1. Scoring the skin: This step prevents the fillet from curling as the skin contracts when being cooked. Make several diagonal, shallow cuts across the width of the fillet.

2. Repeat and make crisscross cuts the other way.

3. Season the fillet with salt and pepper, or other favorite spices.

4. Heat pan at medium high heat. When pan is hot, add a small amount of oil (about 1 tablespoon).

5. Place fillet in the hot pan, skin side down.

6. Cook until skin is crispy and golden brown.

7. Check and turn over.

8. Sauté the fillet to desired doneness.

9. The fillet is ready to serve with garnish and sauce.

PART II

OPEN-OCEAN PELAGIC AND BOTTOM FISH

ʻAhi
Yellowfin Tuna, Big-Eye Tuna

‘Ahi is without question the most prized of Hawaiian fishes. We love it in so many ways—raw in sashimi or poke, grilled or broiled in steaks, lightly seared (as in fried poke), marinated and barbecued or served with a sophisticated sauce in a white-tablecloth restaurant.

The yellowfin tuna is named after its alluring bright yellow dorsal and anal fins. Its flesh is usually a deep red color but can be a light pink in a smaller fish. It turns light gray to white when it cooks, and its texture is steak-like. ‘Ahi is a versatile source of lean protein and an excellent source of EPA, DHA, selenium, magnesium and vitamins B_3, B_6 and B_{12}.

Big-eye tuna is also called " ‘ahi" in Hawaiian. The best quality big-eye tuna is found in Hawaiʻi, especially during the winter season. Big-eye tuna has a higher fat content than yellowfin tuna, which makes the big-eye ideal for sashimi and other raw dishes, although grilling, broiling and sautéing are all popular methods of preparation. Big-eye tuna has a higher EPA and DHA content than both skipjack (aku) and yellowfin tuna and is an excellent source of selenium, magnesium and vitamins B_3, B_6 and B_{12}.

'Ahi Poke Burger with Wasabi Guacamole

Makes 4 sandwiches   *Sharon Kobayashi*

Who says a burger has to be made from beef? Try this.

1 lb.	'ahi, roughly chopped	2 T.	reduced-fat mayonnaise
1 T.	onion, minced	1 clove	garlic, minced
1 tsp.	ginger, grated	2 tsp.	lemon juice
4 tsp.	shoyu	2 T.	green onion, sliced thin (or use
1 tsp.	sesame oil		French chives)
1 T.	sesame seeds	1 tsp.	vegetable oil
1	small avocado, peeled and diced	4	whole wheat hamburger buns
1¼ tsp.	wasabi paste, or to taste		

Optional: shredded cabbage and cucumber slices for garnish

1. In a medium bowl, toss together tuna, onion, ginger, shoyu and sesame oil.
2. Place mixture in a food processor and pulse very briefly. Remove from processor and gently form into 4 (3½-inch) patties (try not to overwork the mixture).
3. Sprinkle both sides with sesame seeds, pressing them in. Freeze for 30 minutes or refrigerate for 1 hour.
4. Meanwhile, make the guacamole by combining avocado, wasabi, mayonnaise, garlic, lemon and green onion. Mix well, mashing the avocado to the consistency desired. Cover and refrigerate till ready to use.
5. Pre-heat a non-stick or cast iron pan on medium-high heat. Add oil and coat the pan evenly. Cook the patties for about 2 minutes on each side, or till the redness in the center just begins to turn pink. Remove immediately.
6. To serve, place on buns and top burgers with an equal amount of guacamole (about 1½ tablespoons), cabbage and cucumber, if desired.

Nutrition Facts

Serving Size (230g)
Servings Per Container

Amount Per Serving

Calories 380   Calories from Fat 140

	% Daily Value*
Total Fat 15g	**23%**
Saturated Fat 2.5g	**13%**
Cholesterol 45mg	**15%**
Sodium 660mg	**27%**
Total Carbohydrate 29g	**10%**
Dietary Fiber 7g	**27%**
Sugars 5g	
Protein 33g	

Pressed Spicy 'Ahi Sushi Squares

Makes 8-10 servings *Carol Nardello*

Making sushi from scratch can be a time-consuming project, but Chef Carol takes a shortcut by making a pan version that's perfect for potlucks.

4 T.	mayonnaise	5 c.	rice (short- or medium-grain
2 tsp.	sriracha chili sauce		"Japanese-style" rice)
1 tsp.	hot sesame oil	5 c.	water
½ tsp.	togarashi seasoning	1½ c.	vinegar
1 lb.	'ahi, diced	¾ c.	sugar
1 T.	tobiko (brightly colored flying fish roe)	1½ tsp.	salt

Black sesame seeds, wasabi sprouts, roasted nori strips, hana ebi (shrimp powder)
or additional tobiko for garnish

1. In a large bowl, mix together mayonnaise, sriracha, sesame oil and togarashi until smooth. Fold in 'ahi and tobiko. Mix until blended. Cover and refrigerate.
2. Cook 5 cups of rice in a rice cooker according to directions. Let rest 5-10 minutes after completely cooked.
3. In a small bowl or measuring cup, combine vinegar, sugar and salt. Stir until sugar dissolves.
4. Place hot cooked rice in a roomy wooden bowl. Pour vinegar mixture on top. Using a rice paddle and a vertical chopping motion, lift and mix rice to coat every grain with the seasoning liquid. Do not stir in a circular motion; fold lightly, lifting and turning, until all liquids are absorbed.
5. Lightly oil a 9- by 13-inch pan and pat half of the seasoned rice into the pan. Evenly spread the spicy 'ahi on top. Cover with remaining sushi rice and press gently. Cover tightly with plastic wrap and chill until needed.
6. Cut into small squares and garnish with black sesame seeds, wasabi sprouts, roasted nori strips, hana ebi or additional tobiko.

Nutrition Facts

Serving Size (409g)
Servings Per Container

Amount Per Serving

Calories 640 · Calories from Fat 70

	% Daily Value*
Total Fat 8g	13%
Saturated Fat 1.5g	7%
Cholesterol 35mg	12%
Sodium 580mg	24%
Total Carbohydrate 118g	39%
Dietary Fiber 2g	7%
Sugars 22g	
Protein 22g	

Pasta Puttanesca with ʻAhi Poke

Makes 4-6 servings

Carol Nardello

8 oz.	prepared ʻahi poke* (not spicy)
1 lb.	bowtie pasta
3 T.	olive oil
2 cloves	garlic, minced
½	onion, chopped
1 can	diced tomatoes (14-oz. can)
1 c.	white wine
3 T.	capers, drained
1 T.	fresh rosemary, chopped (or 1 tsp. dry rosemary)
⅓ c.	kalamata olives, pitted and quartered
1 tsp.	black pepper
1 can	anchovies in olive oil (2-oz.), chopped, reserve oil
2 T.	Italian parsley, chopped

1. Prepare pasta according to package directions. Drain well and rinse with water. Drain any juice from the poke and discard.
2. In a large preheated skillet, pour reserved anchovy oil and olive oil into the pan. Add garlic and onions and sauté until translucent, about 5 minutes.
3. Add tomatoes along with juice, wine, capers, rosemary, olives, pepper and anchovies.
4. Increase heat to medium-high and cook for 3 minutes or until sauce slightly thickens. Add in drained poke and stir until just barely cooked through.
5. Combine cooked poke, sauce and parsley with prepared pasta. Toss well to heat through.

Substitute 2 (5-oz.) cans of tuna packed in water, drained, for poke.

Nutrition Facts

Serving Size (263g)
Servings Per Container

Amount Per Serving

Calories 480   Calories from Fat 120

	% Daily Value*
Total Fat 13g	**20**%
Saturated Fat 2g	**10**%
Cholesterol 20mg	**7**%
Sodium 730mg	**30**%
Total Carbohydrate 63g	**21**%
Dietary Fiber 4g	**16**%
Sugars 6g	
Protein 23g	

Quick Couscous Paella

Makes 4 servings of about 1 cup each   *Sharon Kobayashi*

Paella, the Spanish specialty in which rice and all manner of seafood are cooked together to form a briny melange, is a bit of work. Using couscous instead of rice and bite-size quick-cooking fish saves about an hour of prep time, without sacrificing flavor. Use a fish with good fat content to keep the seafood moist.

12 oz.	'ahi belly, cut into bite-size pieces (or substitute salmon fillet)	2 T.	white wine
¼ c.	salsa	1 c.	reduced-sodium chicken broth
1 tsp.	chili powder	1 pinch	saffron
1 T.	extra virgin olive oil	1 tsp.	salt
½	onion, diced	2 T.	butter, unsalted
½	red bell pepper, diced	1 lb.	asparagus, bottoms trimmed and cut bite-size
1	jalapeño pepper, minced	1 c.	couscous
4 cloves	garlic, minced	1 T.	Italian parsley, minced

For garnish: lemon or lime wedges

1. Marinate fish in salsa and chili powder for 15-30 minutes.
2. Pre-heat a large-ish pot (make sure it can hold 6 cups and has a lid) over medium-high heat. Add oil, onion and bell pepper and saute till onions are translucent (about 5 minutes).
3. Add fish with marinade and cook till liquid is evaporated, and it starts to brown. Add jalapeno and garlic, sauté briefly.
4. Add wine, broth, saffron and salt, and bring to a boil.
5. Add butter, asparagus, couscous and parsley.
6. Stir, cover and remove from heat. Let steam thoroughly for 5 minutes.
7. Gently fluff with a fork before serving.

Nutrition Facts	
Serving Size (370g)	
Servings Per Container	
Amount Per Serving	
Calories 280 Calories from Fat 100	
	% Daily Value*
Total Fat 11g	**17%**
Saturated Fat 4.5g	**23%**
Cholesterol 50mg	**16%**
Sodium 890mg	**37%**
Total Carbohydrate 19g	**6%**
Dietary Fiber 4g	**17%**
Sugars 4g	
Protein 26g	

Chef Carol's Famous 'Ahi Poke

Makes 4-6 pupu servings   *Carol Nardello*

What would any section on 'ahi be without a poke recipe? There are a million of 'em. Here's Chef Carol Nardello's approach, unusual in that she doesn't marinate the 'ahi until serving time.

2 lb.	fresh 'ahi
1 c.	Maui onion, chopped
3 stalks	green onion, sliced thinly
3 cloves	garlic
¾ tsp.	freshly grated ginger
¼ c.	low-sodium soy sauce
½ tsp.	crushed red pepper flakes
1 tsp.	sesame oil
1 tsp.	sriracha hot chili sauce
1 tsp.	Hawaiian sea salt*

1. Dice 'ahi into ½-inch or smaller cubes and chill until needed.
2. In a large glass bowl, combine onions, garlic, ginger, soy sauce, red pepper flakes, sesame oil and sriracha. Mix well and keep this sauce chilled.
3. When ready to serve, combine cubed 'ahi with prepared sauce. Toss well and sprinkle salt on top. Serve on a chilled platter.

* Substitute kosher salt if Hawaiian sea salt is unavailable.

Nutrition Facts

Serving Size (199g)
Servings Per Container

Amount Per Serving

Calories 200   Calories from Fat 30

	% Daily Value*
Total Fat 3.5g	**5%**
Saturated Fat 1g	**4%**
Cholesterol 60mg	**20%**
Sodium 730mg	**31%**
Total Carbohydrate 5g	**2%**
Dietary Fiber less than 1g	**3%**
Sugars 1g	
Protein 37g	

'Ahi Tahini Pita Sandwiches

Makes 5 sandwiches   *Wanda A. Adams*

These Middle Eastern-style sandwiches are very versatile. Though we're stuffing them with a home-made okazu-style fish patty, you can substitute store-bought fish cakes, switch from 'ahi to another fish, or use poached meats or baked tofu. The dressing, a lemon-tahini sauce, is a classic—one you can employ in multiple ways. It's delicious as is, or spice it up with a dash or two of cumin, some hot sauce or harissa, a few shakes of paprika or additional garlic or lemon. If you'd like a more liquid dressing, add water to desired thickness. Though the length of the ingredient list is daunting, this sandwich isn't difficult. The lemon-tahini dressing can be made in advance. The cakes fry up in just a few minutes.

For the sauce:

¾ c.	tahini (sesame butter)
¾ c.	plain yogurt (preferably full-fat, live culture) or Greek yogurt
1 clove	garlic
½ T.	minced parsley
¼ c.	lemon juice (and perhaps a little more)
1 T.	shoyu (soy sauce)

For the salad:

¼	English cucumber, sliced thinly (peeling optional)
1	medium tomato
2 c.	mesclun or spring greens

For the sandwiches:

5	pita breads (6-inch), or flatbreads thin enough for rolling

For the 'ahi cakes:

1 lb.	lower-grade 'ahi, minced
½ c.	mayonnaise
1	egg
1 tsp.	finely chopped garlic
1 tsp.	finely chopped or grated ginger
1 tsp.	lemon juice
7 or 8	finely chopped water chestnuts (optional)
1 c.	panko (Japanese breadcrumbs)
	Vegetable oil for frying

1. Make the sauce: Place sauce ingredients in a blender or bowl and blend until smooth. Taste and correct seasonings. Leftovers can be served over salads, hot grains, with grilled fish. Store in refrigerator in airtight container up to 10 days.

Nutrition Facts

Serving Size (337g)
Servings Per Container

Amount Per Serving	
Calories 680	Calories from Fat 290

	% Daily Value*
Total Fat 32g	**49**%
Saturated Fat 5g	**26**%
Cholesterol 85mg	**28**%
Sodium 580mg	**24**%
Total Carbohydrate 60g	**20**%
Dietary Fiber 5g	**18**%
Sugars 6g	
Protein 39g	

2. Make the 'ahi cakes: Combine 'ahi, mayonnaise, egg, garlic, ginger, lemon juice and water chest-nuts, if using. If the mixture seems too loose, add some panko until the mixture can be shaped into flattish egg shapes (use two serving spoons).

3. Place panko on large, flat plate and lightly toss and press cakes into panko. Heat vegetable oil in medium frying pan and fry patties one at a time until golden brown—2-3 minutes a side, turning only once. Drain on paper towels.

4. Assemble sandwiches: Cut pita breads in half crosswise. Fill each pita with some greens, an 'ahi patty or two, sliced cucumber and sliced tomato.

5. Drizzle with lemon-tahini sauce and serve.

Aku
Hawai'i Skipjack Tuna, Bonito

Assertively flavored, bright red and often sold whole (they average 3-6 pounds in summer and 8-10 the rest of the year), aku are a bit of an acquired taste. If you didn't grow up eating aku bone (aku parts fried in oil with lots of garlic and a splash of vinegar) or aku poke, you may find the taste to be a bit fishy. Aku is usually served raw, as poke, or fried or grilled whole. But we've gathered some ideas here to expand your horizons.

Mature aku are preferable to younger aku because the flesh is a richer, dark red color and has higher fat content, characteristics that are ideal for

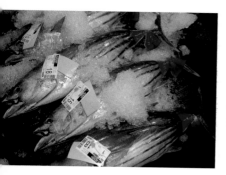

raw preparations. Aku is great for making pupu dishes: poke, dried aku, fried aku bone, tataki-style (seared) and sautéed.

Aku has the lowest EPA and DHA content of Hawai'i's tunas but is still a good source of omega-3 fatty acids. It also is extremely rich in selenium.

Aku and Kale Puttanesca

Makes 4 servings   *Sharon Kobayashi*

Local, vine-ripened tomatoes, good olive oil and fresh herbs make the most of this classic, light, tomato-based dish. Although not traditional, the addition of fish and kale makes the dish more substantial, and the raw onion replaces the cheese usually found in puttanesca.

6 oz.	whole-wheat pasta (about 1-inch-diameter bundle of spaghetti or linguine)	12	kalamata olives, diced small (about 2 ounces)
4 c.	kale leaves (young), sliced	1 T.	fresh oregano leaves, minced (or 1 T. dried oregano)
4 T.	olive oil, extra virgin (divided)		
8 cloves	garlic, minced	1 lb.	aku, diced bite-size (substitute: tombo)
½ tsp.	anchovy paste		
½ tsp.	red pepper flakes (or to taste)	1 T.	fresh flat-leaf parsley, minced
¼ c.	onion, diced	½ t.	pepper, fresh ground (or to taste)
4 c.	tomatoes, chopped in 1-inch chunks	1 tsp.	sea salt
¼ c.	dry white wine		Minced basil, thin-sliced onion, optional
2 tsp.	capers, minced		

1. Bring a pot of salted water to a boil and pre-heat a large skillet over medium-high heat. Add the pasta and kale to the water and cook till the pasta is al dente. Reserving some of the cooking liquid, drain the pasta and kale.
2. Meanwhile, add 2 tablespoons of the oil to the skillet. Add the garlic, anchovy and red pepper, and cook till the garlic is golden brown (about 2 minutes).
3. Add the onion, tomatoes, wine, capers, olives and oregano to the skillet. Cook till the liquid is reduced and thickened (about 5 minutes).
4. Add the fish and cook till the edges just start to turn opaque.
5. Add the pasta and kale and simmer for 2 more minutes, or till fish is just cooked through (add 2-4 tablespoons of the reserved pasta cooking water, if needed to prevent sticking). Be careful not to overcook the fish.
6. Remove from heat and add the reserved 2 tablespoons of oil, parsley and pepper.
7. Add the basil and onion (if using), toss and serve.

Nutrition Facts

Serving Size (464g)
Servings Per Container

Amount Per Serving

Calories 520   Calories from Fat 180

	% Daily Value*
Total Fat 20g	**30%**
Saturated Fat 2.5g	**13%**
Cholesterol 45mg	**15%**
Sodium 830mg	**35%**
Total Carbohydrate 51g	**17%**
Dietary Fiber 10g	**38%**
Sugars 7g	
Protein 40g	

Aku in Saor

Makes 6-8 appetizer servings   *Wanda A. Adams*

If Venice has a national dish, it is sarde in saor—sardines in sour onion sauce (in Italian, "saor" means sour). Versions of this seafood appetizer or first course are found in every restaurant and ciccetti bar (quintessentially Venetian taverns where you can order small nibbles from glass cases, perched on a high chair or standing at a narrow counter along the wall—or even standing out on the sidewalk)—with a glass of Prosecco, a small plate and good friends. Saor is traditionally made with whole, flour-coated fried sardines, but many forms of fish are used, and shrimp is common, too. Saor can be eaten right after preparation, but it's best when aged overnight. As it's usually served at room temperature, it makes a great do-ahead appetizer. Occasionally, saor might serve as a fish course, arranged over hot polenta.

1-1½ lbs.	aku, cut into bite-size squares	1 c.	pine nuts
1 lb.	white onions, thinly sliced and broken into crescents	1 c.	raisins (golden preferred)
		1 T.	pepper
2	bay leaves		Light olive oil for frying
½ c.	white vinegar		Flour

1. Season flour with some salt and pepper and dredge aku pieces until coated on all sides. Set aside. In a large, deep frying pan or Dutch oven, heat olive oil (1-2 tablespoons) over medium heat.
2. Add onions, bay leaves and pepper and simmer, covered 20 minutes or so. The idea is to "sweat" the onions, not brown them; adjust heat or add a few drops water to slow cooking, if needed.
3. Add the vinegar and simmer, uncovered, 5-10 minutes, until reduced. Turn off heat and set aside. In a frying pan, pour in enough olive oil to cover the bottom well. Heat over medium-high heat and fry the aku pieces, allowing them to crisp and brown a bit on each side.
4. In a large, open serving bowl, layer the onion mixture, the fried fish, the pine nuts and the raisins, seasoning as you go with a little pepper. Cover and leave at room temperature if you're eating the dish within four hours. If not, refrigerate and bring to room temperature before serving.
5. Serve with sliced crusty bread or with crostini (garlic toasts).

Nutrition Facts

Serving Size (266g)
Servings Per Container

Amount Per Serving

Calories 480   Calories from Fat 150

	% Daily Value*
Total Fat 17g	26%
Saturated Fat 1g	6%
Cholesterol 45mg	15%
Sodium 105mg	4%
Total Carbohydrate 53g	18%
Dietary Fiber 4g	15%
Sugars 24g	
Protein 34g	

Guava-Glazed Grilled Aku with Roasted Beets and Mizuna Salad

Makes 4 servings   Alan Tsuchiyama

Aku works best cooked rare to medium. Because it has a meatier flavor, Chef Alan here uses a bold glaze that holds up against and complements that big aku punch. Locally grown beets with the spiciness of mizuna are also a nice match for the aku.

2	medium-size beets, peeled and quartered	1 tsp.	finely minced ginger
6 T.	olive oil (divided use)	4 pieces	aku, (4-5 oz. each piece, total 1-1¼ lbs.)
½ c.	pinot noir red wine	1 T.	lemon juice
¼ c.	Hawaiian honey	1 tsp.	rice vinegar
⅓ c.	red wine vinegar	½ tsp.	Dijon mustard
¼ c.	guava juice concentrate	½ tsp.	chopped garlic
1-½ T.	hoisin sauce	1 tsp.	minced shallots
1-½ T.	oyster sauce	2 oz.	baby mizuna*
1 T.	rice vinegar	1	red radish, sliced thin
1 tsp.	chili garlic sauce (optional)		Ground black pepper

1. Place the beets in one layer in a non-reactive oven-proof pan and drizzle with 2 tablespoons of olive oil, pinot noir, Hawaiian honey, red wine vinegar, salt and pepper. Cover tightly with lid or foil.

2. Place in a 350-degree oven for about 1 hour or until cooked — a toothpick can go through the beet with little resistance. Cool beets to a temperature that you can handle and slice beets to desired shape.

3. In a bowl, mix the guava juice concentrate, hoisin sauce, oyster sauce, 1 tablespoon rice vinegar, chili garlic sauce and ginger.

4. Season aku with salt and pepper. Place aku in a bowl and add 2 tablespoons olive oil. Gently mix aku to coat with the olive oil.

5. Grill aku until desired doneness. Just prior to removal of aku from the grill, baste the aku with the glaze.

Nutrition Facts

Serving Size (316g)
Servings Per Container

Amount Per Serving

Calories 460   Calories from Fat 200

	% Daily Value*
Total Fat 23g	**35%**
Saturated Fat 3g	**15%**
Cholesterol 50mg	**17%**
Sodium 690mg	**29%**
Total Carbohydrate 32g	**11%**
Dietary Fiber 2g	**7%**
Sugars 23g	
Protein 34g	

6. In a bowl, mix the lemon juice, 1 teaspoon rice vinegar, Dijon mustard, garlic and shallots.
7. Place mizuna and radish in the bowl and gently toss with the dressing.
8. On the serving plate, arrange one quarter of the mizuna salad. Top with a piece of grilled aku. Drizzle extra guava glaze on top or serve on the side. Arrange the beets on the plate.

Mizuna is a slightly bitter Japanese herb with a peppery taste and pretty notched leaves. Find it at farmers markets, Whole Foods Market or Japanese groceries. Use watercress if mizuna is unavailable.

Hāpuʻupuʻu
Hawaiʻi Sea Bass

Hāpuʻupuʻu, found only in the main island chain and the Northwestern Hawaiian Islands, is a fish with which many are unfamiliar. Homely though the creature may be on the outside, its flesh is dense, white, mild and sweet, and most amenable to a great variety of preparation methods including steaming, sautéing and braising. They're relatively small fish, weighing up to 15 pounds but mostly in the 5- to 10-pound range, plentiful in fall and winter. If you buy or are given a whole one, skin it rather than scaling it; the scales and back fin are sharp and hard to remove, and the skin isn't edible. (Technically, this fish is called hāpuʻu; hāpuʻupuʻu is the name only for the young stage of the fish's life. This is typical of traditional Hawaiians, who often had many names for fish, depending on age, gender, regional differences and so on.) Hāpuʻupuʻu are dark in color, ranging from dark red to black, but their tender white flesh becomes even more tender when cooked.

Cooking tips: Mild in flavor with firm and flaky texture, this fish is ideal for moist heat methods (steaming, braising) as well as stir-frying and batter-frying. Steaming is the most common cooking method. Hāpuʻupuʻu are a good source of EPA, DHA, selenium and vitamins B_3, B_6 and B_{12}.

Braised Hāpuʻupuʻu with Lup Chong, Shiitake Mushrooms and Bok Choy

Makes 4 servings

Grant Sato

While not many types of fish are hardy enough to be braised, hāpuʻupuʻu is an exception. The large flakes of the flesh remain moist and tender when braised.

1 lb.	hāpuʻupuʻu fillet	4	fresh shiitake mushrooms, cut in half
1 T.	salad oil		
2 c.	chicken broth	2	baby bok choy, cut in half lengthwise
2 T.	oyster sauce		
1 tsp.	shoyu	½ c.	julienned lup chong (sweet Chinese sausage)
1 T.	minced garlic		
1 T.	super fine julienned ginger	1⁄16 tsp.	sugar (a pinch)

1. Heat oil in a medium-sized sauté pan on high. When the oil lightly smokes, place the hāpuʻupuʻu fillet skin side up and sear for 1 minute.
2. Turn the fillet over and quickly deglaze pan with the chicken broth. Add the oyster sauce, shoyu, garlic, ginger, mushrooms, baby bok choy and lup chong and allow the liquid to come back to a boil.
3. Once boiling, add sugar and reduce the heat to low, place a lid on the pan, and allow the contents to braise for 10 minutes.
4. Remove the lid and check the fish for doneness.
5. Once the fish is done, it can be served family-style or broken down into individual portions. The accompanying sauce can be thickened with a cornstarch slurry* before serving.

Cornstarch slurry: Add equal amount of cornstarch and water and stir well just before adding. Heat the sauce while adding the cornstarch to cook the starch until smooth.

Notes: Uku may be substituted for hāpuʻupuʻu. Mushroom sauce can be used in place of oyster sauce for those allergic to shellfish products.

Nutrition Facts

Serving Size (677g)
Servings Per Container

Amount Per Serving

Calories 320   Calories from Fat 150

	% Daily Value*
Total Fat 17g	**26%**
Saturated Fat 0.5g	**3%**
Cholesterol 45mg	**14%**
Sodium 970mg	**40%**
Total Carbohydrate 15g	**5%**
Dietary Fiber 5g	**19%**
Sugars 6g	
Protein 30g	

Sweet and Sour Hāpuʻupuʻu

Makes 4 servings   *Wanda A. Adams*

Cantonese-American sweet and sour dishes have fallen out of favor, after an era during which the dishes tended to be loaded with fat in the form of oil-soaked breading on preparations like lemon chicken and sweet-sour shrimp. They were also scarily colored with bright scarlets and yellows that added nothing to their culinary appeal. Here, whole, small hāpuʻupuʻu are steamed in a more balanced, less rich sweet-sour mixture. Have the fish shop dress a 3- to 5-pound fish, yielding at least four 4- to 5-ounce fillets. (Collect the bones and bits for freezing for later use in making stock.)

⅓ c.	apple cider vinegar or Philippines-style coconut sugarcane vinegar (Suka or Sukang Iloco)
⅓ c.	brown sugar
3 oz.	tomato paste (1/2 small can)
4 tsp.	shoyu
⅓ c.	water
1 c.	fresh pineapple, medium-chopped, or 1 (8-ounce) can of pineapple chunks in juice, each cut in half and well drained (reserve the juice)
1 T.	cornstarch or arrowroot
	Freshly ground pepper to taste
4	hāpuʻupuʻu (sea bass) fillets, 4-5 oz. each
	Vegetable oil or olive oil cooking spray
¾ c.	finely chopped mixed bell peppers (green, yellow, orange, red)

Nutrition Facts

Serving Size (301g)
Servings Per Container

Amount Per Serving

Calories 290   Calories from Fat 10

	% Daily Value*
Total Fat 1.5g	2%
Saturated Fat 0g	0%
Cholesterol 45mg	15%
Sodium 580mg	24%
Total Carbohydrate 48g	16%
Dietary Fiber 2g	8%
Sugars 42g	
Protein 26g	

1. Preheat oven to 350 degrees. In a small saucepan over medium heat, whisk together vinegar and sugar until sugar melts; whisk in tomato paste, soy sauce, water, 1-2 T. pineapple juice. Taste; correct sweet-sour balance.
2. Slowly whisk in cornstarch or arrowroot and cook over medium heat until thickened. Reserve, keeping warm.
3. Line a baking dish or pan with foil; paint with vegetable oil or spray.
4. Season fillets with salt and pepper and arrange in casserole or pan.
5. Spoon sauce over the fish. Bake at 350 degrees for 4-5 minutes, depending on thickness of fillets.
6. Remove from oven, scatter pineapple and peppers over fish and return to oven 4-5 minutes or until fish is cooked.

Variations: Instead of baking the fish, season it with salt and pepper, dust it with cornstarch and fry it in vegetable oil; turn once after 5 minutes, pour sauce over, along with pineapple and peppers, and cook until done. In a foil-lined pan, dust pineapple with brown sugar and broil until golden. Add to sauce as directed.

Hāpuʻupuʻu in Aquapazza (Sea Bass with Sun-Dried Tomatoes)

Makes 4 appetizer servings   *Dr. Stephen Bradley*

Sea bass is gently simmered with herbs to form the topping of quick and simple bruschetta (Italian-style appetizer toasts).

4	hāpuʻupuʻu fillets (about 2 lbs. total)
3 cloves	garlic—2 chopped, 1 cut in half
1 bunch	flat-leaf Italian parsley, chopped
¼ tsp.	sea salt
¼ c.	sun-dried tomatoes, chopped
4	large slices rustic Italian bread, toasted until golden brown
	Extra virgin olive oil

1. Place the fish in a large saucepan with 2 chopped garlic cloves, parsley, salt and sun-dried tomatoes. Add water to just cover.
2. Bring to a boil, reduce to a simmer and cook for 15-20 minutes until much of the moisture is absorbed.
3. In the meantime, make bruschetta by toasting the bread slices, rubbing them with the remaining garlic clove halves and drizzling with olive oil.
4. Place each slice in a heated bowl; top with a hāpuʻupuʻu fillet and sauce.

Nutrition Facts

Serving Size (270g)
Servings Per Container

Amount Per Serving

Calories 280   Calories from Fat 30

	% Daily Value*
Total Fat 3g	5%
Saturated Fat 0g	0%
Cholesterol 80mg	27%
Sodium 500mg	21%
Total Carbohydrate 18g	6%
Dietary Fiber 2g	6%
Sugars 2g	
Protein 46g	

Pan-Fried Hāpuʻupuʻu Fillets in Tahini Sauce

Makes 4 servings   *Magdy El-Zoheiry*

Tahini—sesame butter—is a favored ingredient in the Middle East, for both its creamy consistency and its protein yield. Here, chef instructor Magdy El-Zoheiry drizzles a simple lemon-tahini sauce over fried hāpuʻupuʻu fillets (mahimahi, red snapper or tilapia may be substituted).

For the fish:

4 fillets	hāpuʻupuʻu (about 2 lbs. total)
1 c.	all-purpose flour
½ c.	vegetable oil (for frying)
1 tsp.	salt

For the marinade:

2 cloves	garlic, minced
1 T.	extra virgin olive oil
1 tsp.	ground cumin
1 tsp.	salt

For tahini sauce:

1 T.	tahini
¼ c.	warm water
1 tsp.	ground cumin
2 cloves	garlic, minced
1 tsp.	minced curly parsley
1 tsp.	extra virgin olive oil
¼ tsp.	salt
	Juice of ½ lemon
	Chopped parsley for garnish

Make the sauce:

1. In a small mixing bowl, combine tahini and garlic and gradually add warm water, stirring. Add lemon juice, salt and cumin and mix. Taste: you may wish to add more garlic or lemon. Tahini sauce should be neither grainy nor pasty, but in between.
2. Garnish with chopped parsley and reserve.

Marinate and prepare the fish:

1. Rinse fish fillets, then pat dry with a paper towel. Place fish on a large flat plate.
2. In a bowl, combine marinade ingredients, stir and pour over fish, making sure to coat all fillets. Cover, refrigerate for 1 hour.
3. Remove fish from the refrigerator, dry well with paper towel. Dust fillets with flour. Set aside.
4. In a large non-stick pan, heat the vegetable oil on medium-high heat. Add the fillets and fry for about four minutes per side or until cooked. Arrange on a serving dish and sprinkle with chopped parsley. Serve with tahini sauce on the side.

Nutrition Facts

Serving Size (333g)
Servings Per Container

Amount Per Serving

Calories 610   Calories from Fat 330

	% Daily Value*
Total Fat 37g	**57**%
Saturated Fat 4g	**20**%
Cholesterol 80mg	**27**%
Sodium 880mg	**37**%
Total Carbohydrate 28g	**9**%
Dietary Fiber 1g	**5**%
Sugars 1g	
Protein 46g	

Hebi
Shortbill Spearfish

T his sleek, bullet-shaped fish with the grey belly and signature cobalt-blue, body-length upright back fin is softer in texture and milder in flavor than other billfish. It's available year-round and well suited to broiling, grilling or sautéing. It also makes for excellent sashimi and poke. Hebi is a good source of EPA, DHA and selenium.

Whole Grain-Crusted Hebi

Makes 4 servings   *Wanda A. Adams*

Here's an easy weeknight recipe that you can use with many varieties of fish. The secret is to use a rustic and almost gritty whole grain bread, something with lots of nuts and seeds in it, in making the crumbs that coat the fish. Herbes de Provence, the primary flavoring agent, is the taste of the French Mediterranean. It's dominated by thyme, but may also contain savory, fennel, basil, chervil, rosemary, bay leaf, tarragon, marjoram, mint and culinary lavender.

4	hebi fillets, 4 oz. each
½ c.	fresh lemon juice (juice of about 3 medium-to-large lemons)
3 slices	whole grain bread, crust trimmed off, pulsed to crumbs in food processor
1 tsp.	garlic powder
1 T.	onion powder
1 tsp.	Herbes de Provence
	salt and pepper to taste
1 T.	olive oil
1 T.	butter
	Lemon slices for garnish

1. Place hebi fillets in a flat baking dish and drizzle lemon juice over. Marinate two hours, turning once.
2. In another flat baking dish, combine fresh, soft bread crumbs, garlic powder, onion powder and Herbes de Provence.
3. Season fish with salt and pepper. Press the fish into the seasoned crumbs.
4. In a frying pan, combine olive oil and butter and heat over medium heat until butter melts.
5. Place fish in pan and cook slowly until golden. Turn and cook on other side.
6. Serve with a further squirt of lemon juice.

Nutrition Facts

Serving Size (174g)
Servings Per Container

Amount Per Serving

Calories 220   Calories from Fat 70

	% Daily Value*
Total Fat 8g	**13**%
Saturated Fat 2.5g	**12**%
Cholesterol 60mg	**19**%
Sodium 840mg	**35**%
Total Carbohydrate 13g	**4**%
Dietary Fiber 1g	**6**%
Sugars 3g	
Protein 25g	

Calamansi Lime Ceviche

Makes 6 servings   *Sharon Kobayashi*

Calamansi (pronounced kah-la-mahn-see), the Philippine lime, has the flavor of tangerines, adding sweetness and a complexity to any dish. The acid from the lime cooks and tenderizes the fish, resulting in a texture similar to tender scallops. Calamansi develop from green to a bright yellow-orange and are easiest to use and juice when near or at ripeness. Look for them in farmers markets. Ceviche is a raw fish preparation popular throughout Latin America. This recipe offers new ideas for those who enjoy raw fish in Hawaiʻi.

1 lb.	hebi fillet, cut bite-size	½	red bell pepper, diced
¾ c.	calamansi lime juice (approx. 1 lb. limes, or enough to cover fish)	1 tsp.	fresh oregano, minced, or ½ tsp. dried
2 heads	butter lettuce	½ tsp.	ground cumin
2 tsp.	salt	3	small just-ripe avocados (halved, flesh scooped carefully out and diced; save skins for presentation)
1 clove	garlic, minced		
1	jalapeño pepper, minced		
½	onion, diced		

Optional: Minced cilantro, extra calamansi limes cut in half

1. In a zippered plastic bag, combine fish and lime juice. Marinate and refrigerate overnight. Remove leaves from lettuce heads, wash, dry and refrigerate, wrapped in paper towels, until ready to use.
2. Drain most of the juice from the fish, leaving just enough to keep it moist. Transfer fish to a mixing bowl. Add salt, garlic, jalapeño, onion, bell pepper, oregano and cumin; mix to combine.
3. Refrigerate 1 hour to allow flavors to meld. Just before serving, gently fold in avocado.
4. Fill reserved avocado skins with ceviche and place on plates with lettuce leaves to use as wraps for the ceviche.
5. If using, sprinkle with cilantro and serve with extra limes to squeeze over the wraps.

Note: Any billfish, such as aʻu, may be substituted for hebi.

Nutrition Facts

Serving Size (260g)
Servings Per Container

Amount Per Serving

Calories 230   Calories from Fat 120

	% Daily Value*
Total Fat 13g	**21%**
Saturated Fat 2.5g	**13%**
Cholesterol 35mg	**11%**
Sodium 860mg	**36%**
Total Carbohydrate 13g	**4%**
Dietary Fiber 9g	**35%**
Sugars 2g	
Protein 19g	

Hebi with Lavender and Grilled Watermelon

Makes 4 servings   *Alan Tsuchiyama*

Hebi is an excellent fish to grill, and Chef Alan Tsuchiyama likes to eat it at a medium doneness. Hebi is a little softer textured than its cousins nairagi and kajiki and is a species that is gaining popularity with restaurateurs. This is a great outdoor summer dish.

4 pieces	hebi (4-5-oz. each)	4 tsp.	olive oil (divided use)
1 tsp.	Kula culinary lavender	1 T.	lemon juice
3 T.	sweet basil, chopped (divided use)	1 tsp.	salt
2 tsp.	oregano, chopped	2 slices	watermelon, 1 inch thick,
1 tsp.	fresh thyme, chopped		cut 8-inch square
2 tsp.	Italian parsley, chopped	2 T.	balsamic vinegar
1 tsp.	ground fennel seeds	1½ T.	Hawaiian honey
1 tsp.	ground black pepper		

1. In a bowl, mix together the Kula lavender, 1 T. chopped basil, oregano, thyme, Italian parsley, fennel seeds, black pepper, 2 T. olive oil and lemon juice.
2. Place the hebi in the herb mixture and gently turn to coat. Marinate hebi for about 30 minutes.
3. In a small bowl, mix together remaining chopped basil, 2 T. olive oil, balsamic vinegar and salt.
4. Place watermelon on a plate and brush balsamic mixture on both sides. Marinate watermelon for 5 minutes.
5. Remove hebi from marinade and season with salt. Grill hebi to desired doneness. Brush honey on hebi while still hot.
6. On a very hot grill, grill watermelon quickly until lightly caramelized; do not overcook. Cut watermelon into 1-inch squares.
7. Arrange hebi on plates and top and surround with watermelon. Any extra honey and balsamic marinade can be drizzled over.

Nutrition Facts	
Serving Size (194g)	
Servings Per Container	
Amount Per Serving	
Calories 200	Calories from Fat 50
	% Daily Value*
Total Fat 6g	9%
Saturated Fat 0.5g	3%
Cholesterol 55mg	19%
Sodium 730mg	30%
Total Carbohydrate 12g	4%
Dietary Fiber less than 1g	2%
Sugars 10g	
Protein 27g	

Kajiki
Blue Marlin

Lean and flavorful, kajiki is most plentiful during the summer and fall months. In appearance kajiki resembles the nairagi, but it has a less pronounced dorsal fin and its body stripes are not as noticeable. Kajiki also grow much larger than nairagi, sometimes weighing in at more than 1,500 pounds.

Take care not to overcook it, or use moist-heat methods. Yogurt can tenderize and flavor this less fatty fish, and using spice blends can simplify a complicated recipe. Sweet oranges and mango chutney are the perfect complement to this spicy fish. The flesh is best enjoyed when it is derived from smaller kajiki, as the flesh of the larger fish can contain tough and chewy connective tissue. It has a steak-like firm texture, and a slightly rich flavor when smoked, grilled, fried or served raw as poke. Because it contains less fat,

kajiki tends to overcook easily, so check it frequently when cooking.

Kajiki has less EPA and DHA than nairagi but is extremely rich in selenium and the vitamins B_3, B_6 and B_{12}.

Marlin Provençal

Makes 4 servings   *Carol Nardello*

"Provençal" is a cooking term that indicates a dish in the style of Provence, France, meaning lots of bright flavors, fresh herbs and, often, tomatoes.

1 lb.	marlin fillets
1 tsp.	garlic powder
1 tsp.	dried basil
½ tsp.	oregano
2	tomatoes
¼ c.	green olives, sliced
¼ c.	onion, finely chopped
1 T.	olive oil
1 T.	white wine
½ tsp.	salt
¼ tsp.	white pepper

1. Preheat oven to 400 degrees. Lightly oil a 9-by-13-inch baking dish. Place fish fillets in a single layer in prepared dish.
2. In a bowl, combine seasonings and sprinkle half of the mixture on top of fish.
3. Seed tomato: Cut the tomatoes in half, and, working over the sink, squeeze until the seeds pop out. A few seeds aren't a problem. Chop tomatoes.
4. In a medium bowl, combine chopped tomatoes, olives, onions, oil, wine, salt and pepper.
5. Mix until well blended. Spoon evenly over fish.
6. Bake in hot oven for approximately 12-15 minutes or until desired doneness.

Nutrition Facts

Serving Size (221g)
Servings Per Container

Amount Per Serving

Calories 200   Calories from Fat 60

	% Daily Value*
Total Fat 6g	**10**%
Saturated Fat 1g	**4**%
Cholesterol 35mg	**12**%
Sodium 560mg	**23**%
Total Carbohydrate 5g	**2**%
Dietary Fiber 2g	**7**%
Sugars 3g	
Protein 30g	

Ceviche de Pescado (Fish Ceviche)

Makes 4 servings   *Adriana Torres Chong*

Ceviche and its citrus-cooked cousins are a favorite in a number of cultures, from the Caribbean to Tahiti. Here's a Mexican version. Substitute nairagi, hebi or mahimahi if you can't find kajiki.

1 lb.	kajiki, cut in small dice
½	white onion, finely chopped
1	tomato, chopped in medium-size cubes
1	serrano chile, finely chopped (or 2 chiles for spicier ceviche)
3 T.	fresh cilantro, chopped
⅓ c.	olive oil (more, if needed)
1 T.	white vinegar
1 T.	Mexican oregano
½	Hass avocado, cut in slices
	Juice of 5 ½ limes
1½ tsp.	sea salt
	Black pepper to taste
	Corn tostadas (tortilla chips) or saltine crackers

1. In a glass or porcelain bowl, combine kajiki and juice of 5 limes. Refrigerate one hour while acid "cooks" the fish. Strain off lime juice.
2. Stir in onion, tomato, cilantro and serrano chile. Add olive oil, vinegar and juice of ½ lime.
3. Season with salt, black pepper and oregano.
4. Cover and return to refrigerator for at least 45 minutes.
5. Serve in martini glasses garnished with avocado.
6. Arrange chips or saltine crackers separately.

Nutrition Facts

Serving Size (298g)
Servings Per Container

Amount Per Serving

Calories 500	Calories from Fat 260

	% Daily Value*
Total Fat 29g	**45**%
Saturated Fat 4g	**21**%
Cholesterol 35mg	**12**%
Sodium 700mg	**29**%
Total Carbohydrate 29g	**10**%
Dietary Fiber 4g	**17**%
Sugars 3g	
Protein 33g	

Kajiki, Eggplant, Grape Tomato and Long Bean Red Curry

Makes 4 servings

Alan Tsuchiyama

One day, Chef Alan Tsuchiyama was fortunate to receive some kajiki from a friend. He usually sautés kajiki but wanted to try something new and decided to cut it into small pieces and attempt a stir-fry. That night, his family was baffled as to what type of fish was in the stir-fry. He recalls that it was a pleasant surprise to hear the compliments. This recipe proves that kajiki holds up well with this technique. The coconut milk here helps to add moisture to the kajiki.

½ T.	canola oil
2 T.	Thai red curry paste*
1	Japanese eggplant, peeled and cut into bite-size pieces
1 can	coconut milk (13.5 oz.)
8	long beans with ends removed , cut into 2-inch pieces
1 lb.	kajiki, cut into bite-size pieces
1 tsp.	fish sauce (optional)
20	red and/or yellow grape tomatoes
4	lemongrass (bottom portion, white to light green), cut into 2-inch lengths and lightly smashed (use the flat of a Chinese cleaver, large chef's knife or meat tenderizer)
4	Kaffir lime leaves, lightly crushed
40	Thai basil leaves

1. In a skillet or wok, heat the oil and sauté the red curry paste until fragrant.
2. Add the eggplant and cook for a minute, stirring constantly, being careful not to burn the curry paste.
3. Add the coconut milk and long beans. Simmer until eggplant is tender but not mushy or falling apart. Season kajiki with salt and add to curry. Gently stir.
4. Simmer until kajiki is almost done (about a minute or so) and add the remaining ingredients.
5. Remove from heat and serve immediately.

* Curry paste brands are very different, and the degree of spiciness, salinity and flavor varies. Use your personal favorite. Add curry paste in small amounts, stir, taste and correct seasonings again. For a change, you can use yellow or green Thai curry here.

Nutrition Facts	
Serving Size (363g)	
Servings Per Container	
Amount Per Serving	
Calories 380 Calories from Fat 210	
	% Daily Value*
Total Fat 23g	**35%**
Saturated Fat 18g	**91%**
Cholesterol 35mg	**12%**
Sodium 430mg	**18%**
Total Carbohydrate 13g	**4%**
Dietary Fiber 4g	**16%**
Sugars 3g	
Protein 34g	

Tandoori Spiced Fish Salad

Makes 4 entree-size salads   *Sharon Kobayashi*

1 lb.	kajiki fillet, cut into ½-inch thick pieces
½ c.	plain low-fat yogurt
1 T.	lemon juice
¼ tsp.	Liquid Smoke
6 cloves	garlic, minced
½ tsp.	pumpkin pie spice
½ tsp.	cumin, ground
4 tsp.	curry powder
2 tsp.	paprika
1 T.	vegetable oil
1 tsp.	salt
1 T.	cilantro leaves, minced
	Mango Chutney Salad

1. Combine fish with yogurt, lemon, Liquid Smoke, garlic and spices, oil and salt. Allow ingredients to marinate, covered and refrigerated, for 8 hours or overnight.
2. Pre-heat broiler, spray a foil-lined pan with cooking spray.
3. Remove fish from marinade. Arrange on prepared pan with as much space as possible between pieces.
4. Broil till golden brown on top (about 5 minutes). Turn fish over and cook until brown (another 5 minutes).
5. Divide Mango Chutney Salad onto 4 plates, top with fish and sprinkle with cilantro.

Nutrition Facts

Serving Size (267g)
Servings Per Container

Amount Per Serving

Calories 320 Calories from Fat 110

	% Daily Value*
Total Fat 12g	19%
Saturated Fat 1.5g	8%
Cholesterol 35mg	12%
Sodium 680mg	29%
Total Carbohydrate 22g	7%
Dietary Fiber 3g	13%
Sugars 15g	
Protein 33g	

Mango Chutney Salad

Yields ½ cup of dressing

4 T.	mango chutney
2	oranges, peeled and segmented
2 T.	orange juice (reserved from segmenting oranges)
1 tsp.	Dijon mustard
1 T.	shallot, minced
2 T.	vegetable oil
4 c.	spring greens

1. In a small bowl, combine chutney, orange juice, mustard, shallot and oil. Stir till well combined.
2. Just before serving, toss greens with dressing and add orange segments.

Variation: Heat dressing and toss with baby spinach or baby tatsoi for a wilted salad.

Note: Hebi or nairagi may be used in place of kajiki.

Mahimahi
Dolphinfish

Mahimahi is probably the best known fish in Hawai'i, with its sweet, mild, moist white meat that even malihini will try and enjoy. The fillets can be prepared in dozens of different ways—sautéed and served with an elegant sauce, pan-roasted, in stews and curries. A simple idea: Lay fillets on a greased cookie sheet, spread each fillet with a mixture of mayonnaise and wasabi (Japanese horseradish), bake 8-10 minutes at 350 degrees and top with furikake (shredded seaweed condiment). Et voila: furikake mahi!

The mahimahi is a beautifully colored fish with vibrant highlights of green, yellow and blue that extend along the length of the body and dorsal fin. Those caught around the Polynesian islands are regarded as the highest-quality mahimahi in the world. Mahimahi is best eaten fresh, as it does not maintain its appealing qualities when frozen.

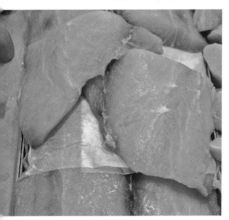

The flesh of the mahimahi is tender and succulent and can be complemented by a variety of spices and sauces. Its texture is on the firm side, but not as steak-like as swordfish. It tastes great broiled, grilled, sautéed or cooked tempura-style. Consumption of mahimahi is an easy way to obtain EPA and DHA omega-3 fatty acids through the diet.

Fish and Corn Chowder

Makes 6 servings   *Carol Nardello*

This is a very delicious and quick-cooking chowder that's ready in less than 30 minutes.

4 c.	clam juice, fish stock or chicken broth
3 slices	bacon, chopped
1	onion, chopped
1 c.	chopped celery
2	potatoes, peeled and diced
2 cloves	garlic, minced
1	bay leaf
1 tsp.	dried thyme leaves
3 ears	sweet corn, kernels removed, or 2 c. frozen white corn kernels, defrosted
2 lb.	mahimahi or other moist white fish
1 tsp.	Old Bay Seasoning
3 c.	fat-free half-and-half
1 T.	butter
1 tsp.	Worcestershire sauce

1. In a medium saucepan over medium heat, bring clam juice, stock or broth to a boil. In a large skillet over medium-high heat, cook bacon until crisp, about 3 minutes.
2. Remove bacon from pan and drain on paper towels.
3. To the bacon fat remaining in the pan, add the onions, celery, potato, garlic, bay leaf, thyme and corn.
4. Stir well and sauté for 3 minutes. Pour in the hot broth and bring to a boil.
5. Reduce heat and simmer.
6. Season the fish with the Old Bay Seasoning and add to the simmering broth.
7. Simmer for about 5 minutes or until vegetables are tender and fish is just cooked through.
8. Add half-and-half, butter and Worcestershire. Heat through and serve piping hot.

Nutrition Facts

Serving Size (584g)
Servings Per Container

Amount Per Serving

Calories 380   Calories from Fat 100

	% Daily Value*
Total Fat 11g	**17%**
Saturated Fat 4g	**20%**
Cholesterol 85mg	**29%**
Sodium 770mg	**32%**
Total Carbohydrate 33g	**11%**
Dietary Fiber 4g	**14%**
Sugars 9g	
Protein 40g	

Almond-Crusted Mahimahi with Red Apple Relish

Makes 4 servings   *Magdy El-Zoheiry*

From Magdy El-Zoheiry, who teaches cooking in the Kapi'olani Community College continuing education program, comes a simple treatment for mahimahi with a slight flavor of the East that would work
as well with other tender, white-fleshed fish fillets. For the red apple relish, use the freshest apple
possible, such as Gala, Corland, McIntosh, Rome, Jonagold, Pink Lady or Fuji. (Red Delicious tends to
be mealy and not cook well.)

For the apple relish:

1	red apple, cored, diced
1	small red onion, diced
1 T.	cilantro plus sprigs, chopped, for garnish
	Juice of 2 limes
⅛ tsp.	salt

1   lemon, cut into wedges for garnish

For the mahimahi:

2	eggs
⅛ tsp.	salt
	Pepper to taste
1 c.	ground almonds
4	mahimahi fillets (4 oz. each)
4 T.	ghee (clarified butter), or olive oil*

1. To make the apple relish: In a small mixing bowl combine apples, onions and cilantro.
   Season with lime juice and salt to taste.
2. To prepare the fish: In a shallow dish, beat eggs thoroughly. Season with salt and pepper.
3. Spread the ground almonds in a flat dish. Dip the fish into the beaten eggs, drain and coat with
   ground almonds on both sides. Set aside.
4. In a large non-stick pan, heat the ghee or oil over medium-
   high heat.
5. Add the coated fillets and cook for two minutes. Reduce heat
   to medium and cook for one more minute.
6. Turn the fillets over and cook for three minutes or until the
   fish is cooked. Do not allow the almond coating to burn. If
   you have to remove the fish before it is cooked to hold for
   some reason, finish it in a pre-heated oven set at 350°F for
   three to four minutes or until it is cooked.
7. To serve, place fillets on a serving dish with the apple relish
   and garnish with lemon wedges and cilantro sprigs.

Nutrition Facts	
Serving Size (262g)	
Servings Per Container	
Amount Per Serving	
Calories 430	Calories from Fat 270
	% Daily Value*
Total Fat 30g	**46%**
Saturated Fat 3.5g	**18%**
Cholesterol 155mg	**52%**
Sodium 280mg	**12%**
Total Carbohydrate 14g	**5%**
Dietary Fiber 4g	**18%**
Sugars 6g	
Protein 32g	

*Ghee can be purchased in Indian grocery stores or you can make it: In a large, deep pot, very slowly melt 1 lb. butter over low heat; skim thick foam, if desired. While the liquid is still clear gold (don't let it brown), remove from heat and carefully pour through 4 layers of cheesecloth into a clean jar. Shut tightly and refrigerate. May be stored for several weeks.

Bruschetta with Mahimahi and Eggplant Caponata

Makes 6 servings (12 bruschetta)   *Sharon Kobayashi*

Sweet-sour caponata (a vegetable stew) is normally served as a side dish. By combining it with mild and tender mahimahi and pungent, fresh goat cheese, it is transformed into a bold-flavored lunch or light dinner worthy of company. You can substitute monchong or butterfish for mahimahi.

2 tsp.	vegetable oil (divided use)	2 T.	balsamic vinegar
¼	onion, diced small	½ c.	water (plus more as needed)
4 stalks	celery, diced	1 tsp.	sea salt
½	red bell pepper, diced	2 tsp.	sugar
1 tsp.	Italian spice blend	1 T.	extra virgin olive oil
¼ tsp.	anchovy paste, or 1 fillet, mashed	12 oz.	mahimahi fillet
¼ tsp.	red chili flakes, or to taste	12 slices	Italian or French bread, ½ in. thick
2 cloves	garlic, minced	1 clove	garlic, sliced in half
12 oz.	Japanese eggplant, diced (about 3 large or 6 small)	6 T.	soft goat cheese such as chèvre
¼ c.	tomato paste		Mix of chopped fresh herbs (e.g., parsley, tarragon, basil, thyme, marjoram), optional
2 tsp.	capers, drained		

1. Pre-heat a large heavy bottom pan (preferably non-stick) on medium-high heat. Add 1 tsp. vegetable oil and sauté fish till cooked through. Remove from heat and cool.
2. Add remaining tsp. of oil, onion, celery, bell pepper; sauté till vegetables softened (about 5 min.).
3. Add Italian spice, anchovy paste, chili, garlic, eggplant and tomato paste. Cook/stir 5 min., or till tomato paste starts to brown.
4. Add capers, vinegar, water, salt and sugar and cook till eggplant is soft and mixture is very thick (about 10 minutes).
5. Using your hands, flake fish into small bite-size pieces and, with a spoon, gently toss with the olive oil and eggplant mixture. Refrigerate until ready to use (can be done the day before).
6. Bring caponata to room temperature before serving.
7. Meanwhile, pre-heat broiler or grill (or use toaster oven).
8. Toast bread on both sides. Lightly rub edges of the toasted bread with the garlic clove.
9. Spread 1½ t. goat cheese on each toast and top with caponata (about ¼ cup per piece). Sprinkle with herbs if using.

Nutrition Facts

Serving Size (284g)
Servings Per Container

Amount Per Serving	
Calories 340	Calories from Fat 90

	% Daily Value*
Total Fat 10g	**15%**
Saturated Fat 3g	**15%**
Cholesterol 30mg	**11%**
Sodium 930mg	**39%**
Total Carbohydrate 42g	**14%**
Dietary Fiber 4g	**18%**
Sugars 7g	
Protein 21g	

Pan-Roasted Mahimahi with Ginger-Garlic Shoyu

Makes 6 servings   *Carol Nardello*

Here, mahimahi is pan-roasted in a classic shoyu-sugar-ginger-garlic glaze.

⅛ c.	low-sodium shoyu
2 T.	sugar
2 T.	vegetable oil
4 cloves	garlic, crushed
2 in.	fresh ginger, sliced and crushed
2 lb.	fish fillets (mahimahi, onaga, ono, wahoo)
4 stalks	green onions, sliced
4	cilantro sprigs

1. Combine shoyu and sugar and mix until sugar dissolves. Set aside.
2. Pre-heat a large skillet on medium-high heat. Add oil, garlic and ginger.
3. Sauté until golden. Add the fillets and brown quickly on both sides.
4. Pour in shoyu mixture and cover pan tightly. Reduce heat to low and simmer for 4 or 5 minutes or until desired doneness.
5. To serve, discard garlic and ginger and place on platter. Sprinkle with green onions and garnish with cilantro.

Nutrition Facts

Serving Size (178g)
Servings Per Container

Amount Per Serving

Calories 200   Calories from Fat 50

	% Daily Value*
Total Fat 6g	9%
Saturated Fat 0.5g	3%
Cholesterol 65mg	22%
Sodium 310mg	13%
Total Carbohydrate 6g	2%
Dietary Fiber 0g	0%
Sugars 4g	
Protein 31g	

Mahimahi Souvlaki with Tzatziki

Makes 4 servings   *Dr. Stephen Bradley*

For this version of a popular light Greek meal, mahimahi replaces beef, lamb or other meats, served with a classic sauce that's half dressing, half salad.

For the souvlaki:

1 lb.	skinless mahimahi, cut into 1-inch cubes
1 T.	freshly-squeezed lemon juice
2 T.	extra virgin olive oil
½ tsp.	dried oregano
¼ tsp.	chopped fresh dill
1 clove	garlic, minced
¼ tsp.	sea salt
¼ tsp.	freshly-ground black pepper
4 pieces	pita (Middle Eastern flat bread), or naan (Indian flat bread)

For the tzatziki sauce:

3 T.	extra virgin olive oil
1 T.	rice vinegar
2 cloves	garlic, minced
½ tsp.	sea salt
¼ tsp.	freshly-ground black pepper
1 c.	Greek yogurt
1 c.	fat-free sour cream
2	Japanese cucumbers, seeded, grated and squeezed
1 tsp.	fresh mint, finely chopped

1. In a small bowl combine olive oil, rice vinegar, garlic, salt and pepper and whisk until emulsified.
2. In a separate bowl, blend yogurt and sour cream; add the olive oil mixture and mix well. Add the grated, squeezed cucumber and chopped mint. Chill for at least an hour before serving; reserve while preparing fish.
3. In a large bowl, mix the fish with the lemon juice, olive oil, herbs, garlic, salt and pepper and marinate for 15-30 minutes.
4. Skewer the marinated fish and cook on a greased grill pan for about 5 minutes a side, until just flaking.
5. Serve on warm flat bread, dressed with tzatziki sauce.

Nutrition Facts

Serving Size (482g)
Servings Per Container

Amount Per Serving

Calories 560   Calories from Fat 210

	% Daily Value*
Total Fat 23g	36%
Saturated Fat 4g	20%
Cholesterol 60mg	20%
Sodium 850mg	35%
Total Carbohydrate 53g	18%
Dietary Fiber 6g	24%
Sugars 8g	
Protein 37g	

Manhattan-Style Fish Chowder

Makes 8 servings   *Carol Nardello*

Chef Carol Nardello has come to prefer this red chowder version over the "thick white kind," since it is lighter and both dairy- and gluten-free.

2 dozen	cherrystone or other hard-shelled clams
5 slices	bacon, chopped*
1½ c.	onion, chopped
1 c.	celery, chopped
2 cloves	garlic, minced
1	bay leaf
1 lb.	potatoes, peeled and cut into 1/2-inch pieces
2 cans	diced tomatoes (28-oz)
1 lb.	mahimahi (or other firm, white fish such as opah or 'opakapaka)
	Tabasco sauce to taste
2 stalks	green onions, sliced
2 T.	Italian parsley, chopped

Nutrition Facts

Serving Size (436g)
Servings Per Container

Amount Per Serving

Calories 260   Calories from Fat 70

	% Daily Value*
Total Fat 8g	12%
Saturated Fat 2g	11%
Cholesterol 55mg	18%
Sodium 470mg	19%
Total Carbohydrate 25g	8%
Dietary Fiber 5g	19%
Sugars 8g	
Protein 24g	

1. Scrub the clams well.
2. In a large skillet over medium heat, bring 1 cup water to a boil. Add clams. Cover tightly and cook 8-10 minutes or until clams open their shells.
3. Transfer cooked clams to a bowl, reserving all cooking liquids. Discard any unopened clams and remove the clams from their shells. Strain the cooking liquid over a large measuring cup. Add enough water to equal 4 cups total. Chop the clams finely.
4. In a large skillet over medium heat, cook the bacon until crisp. Drain cooked bacon paper on paper towels.
5. In the drippings in the pan, cook the onions, celery, garlic and bay leaf. Cook about 8 minutes or until celery softens.
6. Add the cubed potatoes, tomatoes, clams, clam liquid and salt and pepper to taste. Bring to a boil. Reduce heat to low, cover and simmer for 10 minutes.
7. Add the cubed fish and simmer another 5-8 minutes or until potatoes are tender and fish is cooked through. Discard bay leaf and season the chowder with Tabasco sauce to taste.

Bacon is responsible for a lot of the flavor in this dish. To reduce fat and/or cholesterol, use turkey bacon, discard bacon fat and use vegetable oil for sweating vegetables, or omit bacon and use bacon bits made from textured vegetable protein to flavor soup.

Monchong
Sickle Pomfret

Monchong used to be something of an insiders' secret: an inexpensive, moist, tender, white-meat fish that could be used wherever more expensive mahimahi or other fish might be specified. No more—the public has discovered monchong in a big way, and it's now sometimes hard to find.

The monchong is a round-shaped fish with large black scales and short, sickle-like fins. Its flesh ranges from white to light pink in coloring, and although it contains a considerable amount of oil, it has a long shelf life when properly handled.

When cooked, monchong becomes white and firm. It has a pleasant flavor and is especially good for grilling, broiling, sautéeing and baking.

Monchong is an excellent source of selenium and contains a considerable amount of EPA and DHA, the health-promoting omega-3s.

Steamed Monchong with Soy-Ginger Broth

Makes 4 servings   *Alan Tsuchiyama*

Monchong is mild in flavor and contains relatively high healthful oil content. This makes it an excellent eating fish that can be grilled, sautéed, poached, steamed, broiled or baked. Asparagus from Wailua, Kaua'i; fresh hearts of palm and Hāmākua mushrooms from the Big Island make this special. All are available at local farmers markets and some specialty stores.

2 c.	dashi (bonito stock)	4 oz.	Hawaiian hearts of palm, cut into
2 tsp.	soy sauce		sticks about 2 inches long
½ tsp.	sugar	12 stalks	Wailua asparagus, white fibrous
1 tsp.	ginger juice (grate fresh ginger and		bottoms removed, cut into thirds
	squeeze hard with hands)	4 oz.	Hāmākua hon-shimeji mushrooms
4 pieces	monchong (4-5 oz. each)	1 c.	Ho Farms assorted cherry, grape,
2 tsp.	sesame oil (divided use)		teardrop and currant tomatoes
½ tsp.	salt	1 stalk	Tokyo negi* (Japanese green onion),
	Pepper to taste		white part only, sliced very thin
1 tsp.	canola oil	¼ c.	green onion, sliced at a bias

1. In a small pot, bring the dashi, soy sauce, sugar and ginger juice to a simmer. Season broth with salt and pepper to taste.
2. Arrange a steamer over simmering water and place the monchong in the steamer basket. Brush with 1 teaspoon of sesame oil. Season the monchong with salt and pepper and steam for 5 minutes or until cooked.
3. In a skillet, heat canola oil and 1 tsp. sesame oil. Add hearts of palm, asparagus and mushrooms and cook for a few minutes; take care not to overcook.
4. Add tomatoes and Tokyo negi, toss until warmed and remove from heat.
5. Place the vegetables in a soup plate. Arrange monchong on vegetables and ladle soup broth over. Garnish with green onions and serve.

Tokyo negi is a long, leek-like green onion. Can substitute with leek or green onions.

Nutrition Facts

Serving Size (414g)
Servings Per Container

Amount Per Serving

Calories 230   Calories from Fat 50

	% Daily Value*
Total Fat 6g	9%
Saturated Fat 0.5g	4%
Cholesterol 60mg	19%
Sodium 740mg	31%
Total Carbohydrate 15g	5%
Dietary Fiber 3g	12%
Sugars 3g	
Protein 33g	

Pan-Seared Fish-Cucumber Bruschetta

Makes 8 servings   *Kevin Tate*

In this play on a familiar Italian appetizer, healthy cucumber slices replace toasted bread, and mon-chong (or any other fish you might like to try) marries with vegetables for the topping. This rich-tasting dish has an intriguing flavor of Asia due to the use of organic coconut oil (now readily available in many supermarkets). The recipe also makes use of one of Chef Kevin Tate's must-have ingredients: the Cajun/Creole "Holy Trinity" of finely chopped celery, colored sweet peppers and onion. Best made about an hour before serving to allow flavors to blend; do not refrigerate, or coconut oil will solidify.

1 lb.	monchong	2 each	small Roma tomatoes, diced small
	Juice of 1 large lemon (or 2	1	fresh basil (small bunch),
	medium lemons)		chiffonade**
4 T.	organic extra virgin coconut oil*	2 T.	Trinity (recipe follows)
	at room temperature, divided into	½ tsp.	sea salt
	2 T. portions	1	cucumber, sliced evenly at an angle
4-6 cloves	garlic, finely chopped		(16 slices total)

Trinity:
Mince together equal amounts of celery, onion and red, yellow or orange bell peppers (*not* green).

1. Rinse monchong and pat dry. Cut into medium-size pieces.
2. In a large zippered plastic bag, combine juice from lemon and 2 T. coconut oil and marinate fish for about 15 minutes.
3. In small glass bowl, combine remaining coconut oil, garlic, tomatoes, basil, Trinity and sea salt. Set aside.
4. Heat non-stick skillet on medium-high for a few minutes and place in fish with marinade. Saute 2 minutes. Remove from pan and allow to cool.
5. Add to vegetable mixture and break up with fork. Mound on top of sliced cucumbers.

*Extra virgin coconut oil solidifies readily; bring it to room temperature by immersing container in hot water, if necessary.

**To chiffonade, stack leaves, roll them up like a cigar and cut crosswise at desired width.

Nutrition Facts	
Serving Size (133g)	
Servings Per Container	
Amount Per Serving	
Calories 120	Calories from Fat 70
	% Daily Value*
Total Fat 7g	11%
Saturated Fat 6g	29%
Cholesterol 25mg	8%
Sodium 140mg	6%
Total Carbohydrate 4g	1%
Dietary Fiber less than 1g	3%
Sugars 2g	
Protein 12g	

Moroccan Grilled Monchong

Makes 4 servings   *Carol Nardello*

Fragrant spices, citrus and astringent yogurt lend this delicious monchong dish a Middle Eastern flavor.

½ c.	plain yogurt
1	lemon, zested and juiced
1 T.	olive oil
3 cloves	garlic, minced
1½ tsp.	ground coriander
1½ tsp.	ground cumin
¼ tsp.	each salt and pepper
4 pieces	monchong fillets (6 oz. each)
¼ c.	cilantro or parsley, chopped

1. Prepare grill or preheat broiler.
2. Combine yogurt, lemon zest, lemon juice, oil, garlic, coriander, cumin, salt and pepper. Mix to blend.
3. In a flat baking dish, pour half of this mixture over the fillets, spreading mixture over fish, and marinate for 30 minutes. Reserve remaining half of marinade for sauce.
4. Remove fish from marinade and blot dry. Lightly oil the grill and add monchong.
5. Grill or broil approximately 5 minutes depending on the thickness, turning once, until browned on both sides and opaque in the center.
6. Serve with reserved yogurt sauce and sprinkle fresh herbs on top.

Note: Saba or salmon may replace monchong. Substitute mayonnaise if you have no yogurt.

Nutrition Facts

Serving Size (239g)
Servings Per Container

Amount Per Serving

Calories 220   Calories from Fat 50

	% Daily Value*
Total Fat 6g	**9%**
Saturated Fat 1g	**4%**
Cholesterol 75mg	**26%**
Sodium 300mg	**12%**
Total Carbohydrate 6g	**2%**
Dietary Fiber 2g	**7%**
Sugars 2g	
Protein 37g	

Curried Monchong Bites

Makes 4 servings   *Kusuma Cooray*

Professor Kusuma Cooray brings her Sri Lankan flair to this preparation, which can be served as a tantalizing appetizer or as an entree with steamed rice or other grains. She notes that onaga or 'ōpakapaka can replace monchong here, if desired.

For the fish:

2 lbs.	monchong fillets, skin and bones removed
2	fresh green chilies, seeded and finely chopped
1 tsp.	fresh ginger, peeled and minced
1 c.	mint leaves, chopped
2	eggs, whites only
½ tsp.	fresh-ground black pepper
	Sea salt

For the sauce:

1 T.	olive oil
½ c.	finely chopped onion
1 T.	minced scallions, white part only
1 T.	curry powder
⅛ tsp.	turmeric
½ tsp.	cayenne pepper (or to taste)
1½ c.	coconut milk (use lite for less fat)
½ c.	water
1 T.	fresh lemon juice

1. Coarsely mince or chop the fish. In a bowl, combine fish with remaining fish ingredients. Mix lightly and form into 1-inch balls. Place on a dish, cover and refrigerate.
2. To make the sauce, heat oil in sauté pan, add onion and cook gently until golden. Add scallions and spices and cook for 1 minute. Stir in coconut milk and water and bring to a slow simmer; season with lemon juice and additional salt and pepper as needed.
3. Drop the fish pieces into the simmering curry sauce and cook 5-6 minutes until cooked through.

Nutrition Facts	
Serving Size (270g)	
Servings Per Container	
Amount Per Serving	
Calories 300 Calories from Fat 140	
	% Daily Value*
Total Fat 16g	**25%**
Saturated Fat 11g	**55%**
Cholesterol 65mg	**22%**
Sodium 410mg	**17%**
Total Carbohydrate 7g	**2%**
Dietary Fiber 3g	**10%**
Sugars 1g	
Protein 34g	

Monchong Pomodoro

Makes 4 servings   *Wanda A. Adams*

Monchong is delightful—so tender and beautifully flavored. In preparing monchong, editor Wanda Adams usually dredges smallish fillets in cornstarch and quickly fries them, serving them with whatever sauce she feels like making. Her favorite, however, is a fresh, very simple tomato sauce—pomodoro. Substitute mahimahi if desired.

For the sauce:

9 c.	crushed tomatoes (with basil leaf, if possible) or 3 pounds very ripe heirloom tomatoes, peeled, seeded and diced
1 clove	garlic
2 T.	extra virgin olive oil
1 tsp.	sea salt
	Freshly ground black pepper (Tellicherry, if you have it)
	Half a bunch torn fresh basil or 1 T. dried, well-ground with a mortar and pestle

For the fish:

4 pieces	monchong (3-4 oz. each)
	Cornstarch
	Pepper to taste
1 T.	light olive or canola oil
	Minced or snipped flat-leaf parsley

Make the sauce:

1. Prepare the tomatoes if you're using fresh.
2. In a large, heavy pan such as a Dutch oven (e.g., Le Creuset), coat the bottom with the olive oil.
3. Peel the garlic, cut into three pieces and place in pan with olive oil. Simmer over a low flame until the garlic is golden (but *do not* let it burn). Press the garlic with the back of a wooden spoon to release its fragrant esters, and swish the garlic around in the oil. Then fish out the garlic and discard it.
4. Add the tomatoes to the pan all in one swift movement (if you slowly pour, the juices may spit and splatter). Add the salt, pepper and basil. Cook on low, stirring frequently, for 10 minutes or so; then raise the heat to medium and let the sauce cook without bubbling until the water has evaporated and the sauce is kind of jammy. Taste and correct seasonings.

Nutrition Facts

Serving Size (474g)
Servings Per Container

Amount Per Serving	
Calories 290	Calories from Fat 110

	% Daily Value*
Total Fat 12g	**19%**
Saturated Fat 1.5g	**7%**
Cholesterol 50mg	**17%**
Sodium 500mg	**21%**
Total Carbohydrate 21g	**7%**
Dietary Fiber 4g	**17%**
Sugars 9g	
Protein 26g	

Prepare the fish:

1. Sprinkle monchong with salt and pepper to taste. Dredge in cornstarch until coated.
2. Meanwhile, heat 2 tablespoons oil in a frying pan over medium-high heat (hot but not smoking). Fry the monchong pieces until golden brown on both sides; turn only once.
3. Serve topped with a goodly dollop of pomodoro. Or place in a pool of the sauce, if preferred. Scatter minced or snipped flat-leaf parsley over all.

Note: This is particularly nice with a garlic rice or with garlic mashed potatoes. This recipe for pomodoro makes seven cups, so you'll have leftovers to refrigerate or freeze. These go wonderfully with any pasta or can be used as a binder in a casserole.

Nairagi
Striped Marlin

Lean and healthful, nairagi is a good source of vitamins and minerals and low in saturated fats and sodium. It is firm-textured, lending itself to dishes that require a little handling, such as a stir-fry. It can be eaten raw as sashimi or poke, grilled or sautéed. Smoked marlin, sold at many roadside stands, farmers markets and fairs, is a particular treat. Nairagi is best distinguished by its long bill and the light grey stripes that adorn its dark blue body. The best time to enjoy nairagi is during the winter.

Nairagi has flesh that ranges from a light pink to a glowing orange color. It is high in oil and has a long shelf life, which make it ideal for preparation of sashimi poke, and other raw dishes from ceviche to poke. It's also popular smoked, broiled or grilled. When cooked properly, nairagi is firm and moist and has a hearty steak-like flavor and quality. Nairagi is rich in EPA, DHA and selenium, and it also contains high amounts of vitamins B_3, B_6 and B_{12}.

Nairagi Gyros with Tzaziki

Makes 5 servings

Sharon Kobayashi

Usually high in salt and fat, gyros (a Middle Eastern sandwich made from meat cooked on a vertical skewer) is transformed by the use of flavorful, lean billfish. Grinding the fish and mixing it with other ingredients keeps it moist. The aromatic herbs and spices make it possible to keep the salt to a minimum.

4 cloves	garlic
¼	onion, roughly chopped
12 oz.	nairagi, diced
½ c.	fresh bread crumbs
1 T.	lemon juice
1 tsp.	cumin
	Toasted pita bread and fresh tomato slices (optional)
1 T.	Italian herb blend
½ tsp.	black pepper
½ tsp.	salt
1	egg
4 tsp.	extra virgin olive oil
½ c.	cucumber-yogurt sauce

Cucumber-Yogurt Sauce (Tzaziki)

½ c.	plain low-fat Greek yogurt
1½ c.	Japanese cucumber, seeded, sliced thin (about 1 large)
1 T.	onion, minced
2 T.	mint leaves, chopped
2 T.	Italian flat leaf parsley, chopped
1 tsp.	Dijon mustard
½ tsp.	salt
¼ tsp.	pepper

In a bowl or a lidded container, mix ingredients and refrigerate up to 1 hour to let flavors mingle.

1. In a food processor, pulse to mince garlic and onion. Add fish, bread, lemon, spices, salt, pepper, egg and 1 T. oil to processor. Process until ingredients are well combined (about 10 seconds). Refrigerate mixture for 1-2 hours.
2. Pre-heat a large skillet on medium, add remaining 1 T. oil. Use a spatula to spread the oil, evenly coating the pan. Scoop up about 1 T. of fish mixture and form into small patty; fry until brown, turning once, about 4 minutes a side.
3. Serve with Cucumber-Yogurt Sauce.

Note: May substitute other billfish, such as kajiki, hebi or ulua (trevally).

Nutrition Facts

Serving Size (178g)
Servings Per Container

Amount Per Serving

Calories 210   Calories from Fat 70

	% Daily Value*
Total Fat 8g	12%
Saturated Fat 2g	9%
Cholesterol 70mg	23%
Sodium 700mg	29%
Total Carbohydrate 14g	5%
Dietary Fiber 2g	8%
Sugars 3g	
Protein 20g	

Nairagi and Hon-Shimeji Mushroom Lettuce Wraps with Crispy Rice

Makes 8 lettuce wraps   *Alan Tsuchiyama*

The flesh of the nairagi can vary from light pink to orange red. This is a versatile fish that's ideal for sautéing, grilling or deep frying. Lettuce wraps are very popular and fun to eat. This recipe is an interactive meal for a family meal or a party.

	Canola oil for deep-frying	1 T.	shoyu
1 c.	leftover cooked rice, separated*	1 T.	oyster sauce
2 T.	canola oil	1 T.	water
2 tsp.	finely chopped ginger	1 tsp.	sesame oil
1 T.	finely chopped garlic	2 tsp.	sugar
½ c.	chopped onions	2 tsp.	chili bean sauce (or chili bean paste)
1 lb.	nairagi, cut into small cubes	1 tsp.	cornstarch
1 c.	hon-shimeji mushrooms, very coarsely chopped	¼ c.	green onions sliced thin
		½ c.	chopped roasted peanuts
2 T.	sherry or shaoxing wine	½ c.	cilantro leaves
½ c.	water chestnuts, roughly chopped	8 leaves	Island-grown lettuce (e.g., Mānoa
½ c.	bamboo shoots, cut into strips		lettuce), large leaves
1 T.	hoisin sauce		

1. Make the crispy rice: In a deep, heavy-bottomed pot large enough for deep frying, heat canola oil to 350°. Use only enough oil to fill the pot one-third full to prevent boil-over. Don't overcrowd food as you're frying; fry in batches if necessary. Overcrowding the pot causes rice grains to clump; a drop in oil temperature will not allow the rice to puff up and crisp properly.
2. When the rice is puffed and light brown in color, remove from oil and drain on paper towels. Reserve.
3. In a large skillet, heat a little canola oil and fry the ginger, garlic and onions until light brown around the edges. Add the nairagi and hon-shimeji mushrooms and stir-fry for a minute or until nairagi is half done. Add sherry or shaoxing wine and simmer to burn off alcohol.

Nutrition Facts

Serving Size (187g)
Servings Per Container

Amount Per Serving	
Calories 260	Calories from Fat 130

	% Daily Value*
Total Fat 14g	**21%**
Saturated Fat 2g	**9%**
Cholesterol 20mg	**7%**
Sodium 260mg	**11%**
Total Carbohydrate 18g	**6%**
Dietary Fiber 2g	**10%**
Sugars 3g	
Protein 17g	

4. Add water chestnuts and bamboo shoots and stir-fry. In a separate bowl, mix the hoisin sauce, shoyu, oyster sauce, water, sesame seed oil, sugar, chili bean sauce and cornstarch.
5. Add this mixture to the fish mixture while stir-frying. When mixture has thickened, which should take a few seconds, remove mixture from the heat and mix in green onions.
6. Place a lettuce leaf on a plate; fill center with nairagi mixture. Sprinkle crispy rice, peanuts and cilantro on top. Serve.
7. Diners wrap lettuce around nairagi, open wide and enjoy an explosion of flavors and textures.

*Two-day-old leftover rice works the best for frying. When the clumps or rice are easily separated, they fry into individual, oil-coated crisp grains.

Variation: Rice sticks cut into small pieces can be used instead of cooked rice.

Onaga
Hawai'i Longtail Red Snapper

The bottomfish snappers—onaga, 'opakapaka and uku—are the darlings of the white tablecloth set, but this desirability places them at risk of being overfished. Their meat is moist and mild-flavored, and they can be prepared in many ways but especially lend themselves to moist cooking methods.

Onaga is one of the most popular and highly valued fish in Hawai'i, especially among Japanese visitors, who consider its brilliant red color to be good luck. Like most fish, onaga is best enjoyed during the winter months, as fish that are harvested in winter typically have higher fat content than those caught in the summer.

Delicate flavored and moderately firm textured, onaga can be prepared in a multitude of ways, including raw dishes from ceviche to poke. It is also popular smoked, broiled or grilled.

Onaga is a rich source of EPA and DHA; a 4 oz. portion will provide more than the recommended daily amounts of EPA and DHA established by the American Dietetic Association.

Day-Boat Onaga with Pacific Oysters

Makes 2 servings   *George Mavrothalassitis*

Chef George Mavrothalassitis has made this fish his signature item with his menu favorite, onaga, baked in a salt crust. Don't be put off by the lengthy ingredient list. The techniques required are really very simple: Blanched radicchio forms a bed for sauteed fish. A baked oyster goes on top, followed by a puree of cilantro and then a simple oyster-onion sauce.

For the garnish:

1 bunch	radicchio (small bunch)
1 c.	white wine
1 T.	extra-virgin olive oil
2	Pacific oysters, medium size
½ T.	extra virgin olive oil

For the oyster velouté sauce:

2	Pacific oysters, medium size
½ c.	Maui onion puree (last step below)
½ tsp.	garam masala
½ T.	extra virgin olive oil

For the essence of cilantro:

1 c.	cilantro leaves
½ c.	Maui onion puree (recipe follows)

For the fish:

1 T.	Extra virgin olive oil
2 pieces	onaga fillets (6 oz.)
	Sea salt
	Ground white pepper or peppercorn from the pepper mill, to taste

1. Blanch the radicchio in boiling salted water, plunge into ice water.
2. Cut the radicchio in half, season with salt and pepper and bake for 15 minutes in 1 c. of white wine, reserve.
3. Bake all four oysters in the shell in a 400° oven, cool in ice water, shuck the oysters, making sure you remove all pieces of shell from the oyster meat. Reserve 2 pieces for the sauce and 2 pieces for the garnish.
4. Oyster velouté: Bring half of the onion puree to a boil, place the puree in the blender, add two of the oysters, blend at high speed, season with the garam masala, finish with olive oil. Pass through a fine chinois. Set aside.
5. Essence of cilantro: Blanch the cilantro in boiling salted water, cool in ice water. Strain the cilantro and blend with the rest of the onion puree, olive oil and salt and pepper as desired.
6. Using a non-stick frying pan, sauté in olive oil the onaga fillets skin-side down, start at low heat then increase the temperature until the skin is crispy, finish cooking at 350°.
7. On serving plates, place the radicchio in the center, arrange fish fillet on top, then baked oyster on each.
8. Cover the oyster with the essence of cilantro. Surround the dish with the oyster velouté.
9. Maui onion puree: Finely slice 1 Maui onion, simmer in white wine for 1 hour, puree in blender.

Nutrition Facts

Serving Size (513g)
Servings Per Container

Amount Per Serving

Calories 570   Calories from Fat 260

	% Daily Value*
Total Fat 29g	**44%**
Saturated Fat 5g	**25%**
Cholesterol 120mg	**39%**
Sodium 260mg	**11%**
Total Carbohydrate 14g	**5%**
Dietary Fiber 1g	**5%**
Sugars 3g	
Protein 44g	

Grilled, Lettuce-Wrapped Onaga with Tokyo Negi

Makes 4 servings

Sharon Kobayashi

Onaga is delicate in flavor and texture, so it's difficult to grill. Wrapping the fish in lettuce protects it, keeping the moisture in while adding a subtle smoky flavor. This is a very good use for the outer leaves of a head of romaine, which are usually otherwise discarded. Tokyo negi (a leek-like green onion) is very sweet roasted or sautéed and complements the subtle flavor of onaga. You can find it at the Hawaii Farm Bureau Federation's farmers markets, Marukai or Whole Foods Market.

1 c.	thin-sliced Tokyo negi, white parts	1 lb.	onaga fillet, cut into 4½-inch pieces
2 tsp.	butter, unsalted	½ tsp.	pepper
¼ tsp.	sea salt	1 tsp.	thyme leaves, fresh, minced
8	romaine lettuce, large leaves	1 tsp.	oil for brushing

1. Sauté Tokyo negi in butter on medium heat until very soft (about 10 minutes).
2. Meanwhile, bring a pot of water to a boil. Add lettuce leaves and cook for 10 seconds. Remove leaves, drain and cool. Pat leaves dry, trim tough ends (about bottom 2 inches).
3. Lay 2 leaves side-by-side, overlapping by one-third. Spread one quarter of leek mixture in the middle. Lay one onaga fillet over leeks, and sprinkle with ¼ tsp. salt, pepper and thyme to taste.
4. Roll up leaves to cover fish tightly (like a burrito). Brush with oil.
5. Grill for 7-8 minutes on each side, till lettuce has a nice brown color.

Roasted Pepper Vinaigrette (Makes 8 servings)

1	sweet red bell pepper, roasted, peeled and seeded (8 oz. if using prepared)
1-2 cloves	garlic
2 T.	sliced almonds, toasted
1 T.	red wine vinegar
½ tsp.	sea salt
½ tsp.	pepper
3 T.	extra virgin olive oil

1. Combine pepper, 1 clove garlic, almonds, vinegar, salt and pepper in a blender.
2. Blend till smooth. With blender running, drizzle in olive oil. Add more garlic if desired.

Nutrition Facts

Serving Size (199g)
Servings Per Container

Amount Per Serving

Calories 230   Calories from Fat 120

	% Daily Value*
Total Fat 13g	**20%**
Saturated Fat 3g	**16%**
Cholesterol 50mg	**17%**
Sodium 500mg	**21%**
Total Carbohydrate 6g	**2%**
Dietary Fiber 1g	**6%**
Sugars 2g	
Protein 23g	

Spicy Fish Soup

Makes 8-12 servings

Kevin Tate

In this soup, Chef Kevin Tate gets his Cajun mojo going. Don't be afraid of the amount of spice; this soup does light up your tongue a bit, but not so much that the average person can't handle it. We've used snapper here, but you can choose any flaky fish. Don't overcook the fish and be gentle as you flake it. Avoid stirring the soup too much before serving. A crusty, country-style bread completes the experience. Spicy Spaghetti Seasoning, with Italian herbs, dried onions and spices, is a commercial product that Tate uses in many of his dishes.

4 T.	extra virgin olive oil	2 T.	Spicy Spaghetti Seasoning
2 T.	Cajun Spice (recipe follows)	2 T.	hot pepper sauce (preferably a
1 lb.	onaga, filleted		Louisiana hot pepper sauce such as
2 cans	stewed tomatoes (14.5-oz. each,		Crystal, and not Tabasco)
	organic or good-quality Italian-style	½ tsp.	Worcestershire sauce
	stewed tomatoes), chopped or pulsed	2 cups	Trinity: Mince together equal
	in food processor		amounts of celery, onion and red,
8 c.	vegetable broth/stock, low sodium		yellow or orange bell peppers

1. Mix oil and Cajun Spice in large zippered plastic bag. Marinate fish fillets for 10 minutes. Broil fish in foil-lined pan, 3 minutes each side; set aside to cool.

2. In medium stock pot, combine tomatoes, water, Spicy Spaghetti Seasoning, vegetable broth, hot pepper sauce and Worcestershire sauce. Bring to a simmer for about 15 minutes to incorporate flavors.

3. Gently flake fish with fork or by hand. Add fish and Trinity and simmer on low 10 minutes. Taste and correct seasonings; if too spicy, add ½ cup water, if more spice is desired, add Cajun Spice to your own bowl. Serve hot.

Cajun Spice:

		½ tsp.	thyme
½ tsp.	garlic powder	½ tsp.	oregano
½ tsp.	onion powder	¼ tsp.	cayenne
½ tsp.	paprika	¼ tsp.	black pepper

Blend and use as desired. Double or triple the ingredients and store in an airtight container in your spice cupboard.

Nutrition Facts

Serving Size (698g)
Servings Per Container

Amount Per Serving

Calories 220   Calories from Fat 90

	% Daily Value*
Total Fat 10g	**15%**
Saturated Fat 2g	**10%**
Cholesterol 25mg	**8%**
Sodium 630mg	**26%**
Total Carbohydrate 21g	**7%**
Dietary Fiber 3g	**12%**
Sugars 7g	
Protein 14g	

Baked Onaga with Tomatoes and Homemade Harissa

Makes 4 servings   *Magdy El-Zoheiry*

While we're in spicy mode, harissa is the chili sauce of the Moroccan people. It's unlike other chili sauces so you'll need to buy it or make it yourself, as outlined in the recipe here from cooking teacher Magdy El-Zoheiry, who is originally from Alexandria, Egypt.

For the fresh harissa:

4-6	dried small, hot, red chilies, stems removed*
1 T.	ground coriander
1 T.	ground cumin
1 tsp.	dried mint
1 tsp.	ground caraway seeds
5 cloves	garlic
½ c.	olive oil

For the fish:

2-2½ lbs.	whole onaga, scaled and cleaned
1 T.	harissa (Moroccan chili paste)
3 T.	extra virgin olive oil
4 cloves	garlic, crushed
2	sliced lemons
1	Maui sweet onion, large, sliced
2	tomatoes, large, ripe, sliced
3 sprigs	Italian parsley
3 sprigs	fresh thyme

* Use Japanese dried chilies or any medium-hot chili such as Szechuan chilies or chile de arbol.

Make the harissa:

1. Using scissors or a sharp knife, cut chilies into pieces. Cover with boiling water and cook to soften, 30-90 minutes. Drain chilies and squeeze out excess water.
2. Place chilies in food processor with remaining harissa ingredients. Grind to a paste. Scrape down sides, then process again for 20 seconds. Place in small glass jar (it will soak into and stain many plastic containers). Cover surface with thin layer of olive oil; seal tightly. Harissa keeps in the refrigerator for up to 8 weeks; wonderful in soups, sauces, stews.

Nutrition Facts	
Serving Size (457g)	
Servings Per Container	
Amount Per Serving	
Calories 440 Calories from Fat 190	
	% Daily Value*
Total Fat 22g	**33%**
Saturated Fat 4g	**21%**
Cholesterol 100mg	**34%**
Sodium 220mg	**9%**
Total Carbohydrate 16g	**5%**
Dietary Fiber 5g	**18%**
Sugars 4g	
Protein 52g	

Prepare the fish:

1. Pre-heat oven to 400°. Wash fish under running water for two minutes, making sure to remove all surface blood. Dry the fish well with paper towels.
2. Make two to three diagonal slashes on each side of the fish to ensure even cooking. In a small bowl, combine harissa, olive oil and garlic. Rub harissa mixture on both sides of fish and cavity.
3. Lightly grease a baking dish large enough to hold the whole fish, then arrange the sliced onion on the bottom. Arrange tomatoes, parsley, thyme and sliced lemons over onions.
4. Place fish on top and bake uncovered for 35-40 minutes or until the fish is cooked.
5. Serve hot with French bread (baguette).

Ono
Wahoo

Sleek, powerful ono are prized game fish, both because they put up a good fight and because the rich-tasting white flesh is well worth the effort. Canned wahoo from the South Pacific has enjoyed a rather faddish popularity in Hawai'i the past few years, since Samoans and others started bringing cans to the Hawaiian Islands as gifts and local stores then began to stock it. Pricey, but again, well worth it. Ono, the fish, is 'ono (delicious); a diacritical mark differentiates them.

Ono has a delicate texture—flaky and mild flavored. Moist heat methods are best, but a tempura preparation also works well, to add richness.

Although ono is considered a lean fish, it nonetheless provides a significant amount of EPA and DHA. Ono is also an excellent source of selenium and vitamins B_3, B_6 and B_{12}.

Ono in a Creamy Tahini Sauce

Makes 4 servings   *Sharon Kobayashi*

This is a very tasty and easy-to-prepare variation of creamed tuna. The most difficult part is finding sumac, a Middle Eastern spice (try specialty stores such as Oliver's in Kāhala or purchase online) with a tart, earthy and floral flavor.

1 tsp.	olive oil
1 each	onion, diced
2 tsp.	cumin
1 tsp.	sumac
1-¼ tsp.	sea salt
2 c.	water
2 tsp.	tahini (sesame butter)
2 tsp.	lemon juice
1 lb.	ono fillet, cut bite-size

1. In a heavy-bottomed skillet, sauté onion in oil. Cook over medium-low heat, stirring occasionally, till the onions are a deep brown (about 15 minutes).
2. Add cumin and cook for 2 minutes. Add sumac, salt and water. Stir in tahini and lemon juice.
3. Add fish and cook for 5 minutes, or till fish is opaque and firm. Add more water if sauce gets too thick.

Note: If you just can't find sumac, use ume paste—the seedless paste of the Japanese pickled plum. Tombo 'ahi may be substituted.

Nutrition Facts

Serving Size (271g)
Servings Per Container

Amount Per Serving

Calories 170   Calories from Fat 50

	% Daily Value*
Total Fat 6g	**9**%
Saturated Fat 0.5g	**3**%
Cholesterol 55mg	**18**%
Sodium 740mg	**31**%
Total Carbohydrate 4g	**1**%
Dietary Fiber less than 1g	**4**%
Sugars 1g	
Protein 27g	

Ono alla Olive with Swiss Chard

Makes 4 servings   *Dr. Stephen Bradley*

Here sautéed onion is topped with a chunky, brightly flavored mixture and served over healthful Swiss chard.

2 lbs.	ono	1 T.	capers
2 cloves	garlic, minced	¼ c.	kalamata olives, pitted
5 T.	extra virgin olive oil	10	cherry tomatoes
2	bay leaves	2 T.	flat-leaf parsley, chopped
¼ tsp.	sea salt	12 leaves	Swiss chard
¼ tsp.	freshly ground black pepper	1 T.	toasted pine nuts

1. Divide the fish into 4 even pieces and place in a non-reactive bowl. Add 1 clove garlic, 2 T. olive oil, bay leaves, salt and pepper. Mix well and allow to marinate for about 1 hour.
2. Slice the tomatoes into 4 pieces. In a large skillet, heat 2 T. olive oil over medium heat. Add tomatoes, capers, parsley and olives and sauté for 2 minutes.
3. Move the tomato mixture to one side of the pan, arrange the fish in the pan and spoon tomato mixture over each piece. Allow to cook for 5 minutes undistorbed, then, again, move the sauce to the side, turn the fish gently and spread with tomato mixture. Lower heat to medium-low, cover the pan and cook another 10 minutes.
4. Remove bay leaves and reserve while preparing vegetables.
5. In another skillet, over medium heat, briefly sauté the remaining clove of garlic in 1 T. olive oil (be careful not to brown the garlic, as it will turn bitter).
6. Add the Swiss chard leaves and allow to cook for 2 minutes until greens are just wilted.
7. On heated plates, place 3 leaves of chard and one portion of ono, spoon over some of the sauce and sprinkle the pine nuts on top.

Nutrition Facts

Serving Size (453g)
Servings Per Container

Amount Per Serving

Calories 470   Calories from Fat 230

	% Daily Value*
Total Fat 25g	**39%**
Saturated Fat 3g	**15%**
Cholesterol 110mg	**37%**
Sodium 950mg	**39%**
Total Carbohydrate 10g	**3%**
Dietary Fiber 3g	**13%**
Sugars 3g	
Protein 56g	

Ono Provençal

Makes 6 servings   *Dr. Stephen Bradley*

Here ono adds a bit of heft to a quick version of a ratatouille-like vegetable stew.

1 T.	extra-virgin olive oil
2 cloves	garlic, sliced
2½ c.	red onion, finely sliced
½ tsp.	sea salt (divided into two portions, ¼ tsp. each)
1 can	chopped peeled plum tomatoes with their juice
1¾ c.	thinly sliced fennel bulb (about 1 small bulb)
1 c.	dry white wine (e.g., sauvignon blanc)
⅓ c.	chopped fresh basil
¼ c.	chopped, pitted kalamata olives
1 T.	tomato paste
⅛ tsp.	crushed red pepper
2 tsp.	capers
1	bay leaf
¼ c.	water
⅛ tsp.	freshly ground black pepper
6	ono fillets (6 oz. each)

1. Preheat oven to 450°.
2. Heat oil in a large ovenproof skillet over medium-high heat, add garlic. Cook 30 seconds, stirring constantly; add onion and ¼ tsp. salt. Cook for 2 minutes, stirring occasionally.
3. Add tomato and next 10 ingredients (fennel through black pepper) and cook on stovetop for 10 minutes.
4. Place fish fillets on top of mixture, transfer to oven and cook for 10 minutes or until fish flakes easily when tested with a fork. Discard bay leaf before serving.

Nutrition Facts

Serving Size (366g)
Servings Per Container

Amount Per Serving

Calories 290   Calories from Fat 60

	% Daily Value*
Total Fat 7g	**10%**
Saturated Fat 0.5g	**3%**
Cholesterol 85mg	**28%**
Sodium 550mg	**23%**
Total Carbohydrate 13g	**4%**
Dietary Fiber 3g	**11%**
Sugars 4g	
Protein 41g	

Opah
Moonfish

The first time you encounter a large opah—at a food festival or perhaps at the fish auction—you'll think you've suddenly been transported to another planet. Here is this impossibly large, impossibly round, gorgeously colored creature—white polka dots over a rosy pink background. They can weigh as much as 200 pounds. And they are some good eatin'.

Opah is very versatile. Its flesh is firm-textured, with an appealing flavor that can be enjoyed year-round. Because of its high fat content, it is good for almost any cooking method, including raw as sashimi, sautéed, as fried poke, baked or grilled.

Opah are more than just beautiful fish. They are extremely rich in

EPA and DHA, containing more than double or even triple the amounts of omega-3 fatty acids found in other species of fish. Significant amounts of selenium and the vitamins B_3, B_6 and B_{12} are also present in opah.

Opah and Apple Banana en Papillote

Makes 4 servings   *Sharon Kobayashi*

Apple bananas that are mostly yellow with a hint of green feature a balance of sweet, sour and starch that is perfect for this dish. Ti leaf imparts a subtle flavor, and coconut milk adds a little richness and moisture. If opah is not available, substitute a mild-flavored white-flesh fish, such as mahimahi or tilapia. The presentation of the parchment-wrapped fish is impressive, and it's as easy to do for one person as for eight. In the absence of kitchen parchment, use foil. In that case, position the fish so the packet opens from the top (like a purse).

For the fish:

4	apple bananas, large, not quite ripe, sliced thin and mashed slightly
2 tsp.	curry powder
2 T.	teriyaki sauce (store-bought or homemade)
4 T.	coconut milk (preferably frozen)
1 lb.	opah, cut into 4½-inch thick fillets
4	very thin slices lemon
4 sprigs	cilantro (optional)

For the wrapping:

4 pieces	ti leaves (or banana leaves), cut into 7-inch-by 5-inch rectangles
4 sheets	parchment paper, cut into 16-inch-by-12-inch rectangles (or substitute aluminum foil)
	Vegetable oil

1. Pre-heat oven to 350 degrees.
2. Fold parchment in half to make an 8-inch-by-12-inch rectangle, crease it and unfold. Lightly oil the paper. Place a leaf on one side of the crease, centering it.
3. Arrange 1 sliced banana in a thin layer over each leaf, covering it.
4. Sprinkle with ½ T. curry, ½ T. teriyaki sauce and 1 T. coconut milk. Place fillet over bananas and drizzle with 1 T. teriyaki sauce, rubbing it in.
5. Lay 1 lemon slice and cilantro sprig (if using) on each. Fold paper over fish. Starting at one end, fold closed using a rolling motion, crimping down firmly as you go.
6. The shape should resemble a turnover (half circle). Turn the last edge under and pinch. Repeat for remaining fillets.
7. Arrange packets on a baking sheet, and bake for 25 minutes. To serve, place a packet on each plate, cut open with a sharp knife. Remove lemon and cilantro before eating.

Nutrition Facts

Serving Size (229g)
Servings Per Container

Amount Per Serving

Calories 290   Calories from Fat 100

	% Daily Value*
Total Fat 12g	**18%**
Saturated Fat 5g	**27%**
Cholesterol 60mg	**20%**
Sodium 430mg	**18%**
Total Carbohydrate 22g	**7%**
Dietary Fiber 3g	**12%**
Sugars 11g	
Protein 26g	

Baja Fish Taco

Makes 4 servings

Adriana Torres Chong

Chef Adriana Torres Chong teaches popular Mexican cooking courses in the Kapi'olani Community College non-credit curriculum. Here's a favorite dish that can be an antojito (appetizer) or entree. (Substitute mahimahi if you can't find opah.)

1⅓ c.	all-purpose flour
½ tsp.	sea salt
	Pepper to taste
1 c.	beer
1⅓ lb.	opah fillet, cut into ½-inch strips
1	lime

For the sauce:

1	smoked chipotle chile, finely chopped (for less heat, use half chile)
1 clove	garlic, finely chopped
⅔ c.	crema Mexicana (Mexican cream)*
¼ tsp.	sea salt
	Pepper to taste

For the fish:

12	corn tortillas
	Vegetable oil for deep frying

For the garnish:

1	lime, cut into quarters
1 c.	diced tomato
1 c.	red cabbage, thinly sliced

1. Make the batter: Whisk flour, salt and pepper; add beer, mix thoroughly and let the batter sit 15 minutes in refrigerator.
2. Sprinkle fish with salt and pepper. Squeeze some lime juice over each strip, marinate 5 minutes. Place in batter.
3. Make sauce: Mix all ingredients and seasonings. Fry fish: Heat vegetable oil to 350 degrees in heavy saucepan.
4. Place battered fish strips in hot oil and fry until golden-brown. Reheat tortillas.
5. Fill each tortilla with fried fish strips and top with sauce and garnish. Serve immediately.

* May substitute Mexican cream with sour cream mixed with a dash of milk and a pinch of salt.

Nutrition Facts

Serving Size (467g)
Servings Per Container

Amount Per Serving

Calories 660   Calories from Fat 210

	% Daily Value*
Total Fat 24g	**36%**
Saturated Fat 11g	**53%**
Cholesterol 120mg	**40%**
Sodium 840mg	**35%**
Total Carbohydrate 68g	**23%**
Dietary Fiber 7g	**28%**
Sugars 4g	
Protein 41g	

Grilled Opah Belly on Wilted Arugula and Macadamia Nuts with Island Salad

Makes 4 servings   *Alan Tsuchiyama*

Opah is one of the best Hawaiian fish in the sea. It is tasty, very forgiving in cooking, very nutritious, full of omega-3 fatty acids and usually available year-round. Due to its high fat content, opah belly is good for grilling.

2 ears	sweet corn in husk, Hawai'i grown	½ tsp.	smoked paprika
½ c.	rough-chopped sea asparagus*	1 tsp.	salt
1	radish, sliced very thin		Black pepper to taste
¼ c.	small diced red onion	4 pieces	opah belly, 4–5 oz. each
1 T.	chopped cilantro	1 T.	lemon juice
1 T.	olive oil	1 T.	macadamia nut oil
1 T.	lime juice	4 oz.	arugula
½ tsp.	ground cumin	¼ cup	roasted macadamia nuts

1. On a hot grill, place the ears of corn with husks on. Grill in the husks for about 20-30 minutes until the corn is cooked. The husk may start to get brown, but don't worry—the corn will be fine.
2. When corn is done, remove husk and silk (corn hairs). Stand the corn up in a deep bowl and run sharp knife from top to bottom to remove kernels. Do not cut too deep, or it will get very fibrous.
3. In a bowl, mix the roasted corn kernels, sea asparagus, radish, red onion, cilantro, olive oil, lime juice, cumin, smoked paprika, salt and pepper together and set aside.
4. Season the opah belly with salt, pepper and lemon juice. Grill opah belly until just done and remove from heat. In a sauté pan, heat the macadamia nut oil and wilt the arugula.
5. Season the arugula with salt and pepper and mix in roasted macadamia nuts.
6. Place the arugula on a plate, then place the opah belly over arugula and top it off with a serving of sea asparagus, roasted island-grown sweet corn and radish salad.

* Sea asparagus, sometimes called sea bean, is a branched green sea plant, crisp, salty and bursting with moisture, grown in Kahuku aquaculture beds. You can find it at the KCC Farmers Market and at some specialty food stores. It can be eaten raw, tossed into stir-fries or pickled. We've even seen sea asparagus sushi!

Nutrition Facts

Serving Size (254g)
Servings Per Container

Amount Per Serving

Calories 370   Calories from Fat 210

	% Daily Value*
Total Fat 23g	**36%**
Saturated Fat 5g	**25%**
Cholesterol 70mg	**23%**
Sodium 710mg	**30%**
Total Carbohydrate 14g	**5%**
Dietary Fiber 3g	**13%**
Sugars 3g	
Protein 31g	

Baked Opah with Mustard Sauce

Makes 4 servings   *Eddie Fernandez*

Simply baked, then served over a bed of vegetables, opah here makes an easy supper for company.

4	opah fillets (10 oz. each)
¼ tsp.	kosher salt
	Black pepper to taste
9 oz.	sour cream (reduced-fat is fine)
3 T.	Dijon mustard
2 T.	whole-grain mustard
2 T.	shallots, minced
1½ T.	capers, drained
4 pieces	baby bok choy, rinsed and sliced in half lengthwise
4 oz.	hon-shimeji mushrooms, stems removed
4 oz.	shelled edamame (soybeans)
2 T.	sesame oil

1. Pre-heat oven to 425°F.
2. Place fish fillets in an ovenproof baking dish and sprinkle with salt and pepper both sides.
3. In a small mixing bowl, combine the sour cream, Dijon mustard and whole grain mustard, shallots, capers and mix well. Spoon sauce evenly over each fish fillet.
4. Bake in a 425°F oven for about 8-10 minutes or until the fish is barely done (timing depends on thickness of fish fillets).
5. In a large sauté or frying pan, add the sesame oil and heat until hot. Add the bok choy, mushrooms and beans and season with salt and pepper. Sauté for about 2 minutes until vegetables are lightly cooked but still crunchy.
6. Arrange an even amount of vegetables in the center of four plates. Place opah fillet on each.

Nutrition Facts

Serving Size (454g)
Servings Per Container

Amount Per Serving	
Calories 700	Calories from Fat 360

	% Daily Value*
Total Fat 40g	**62%**
Saturated Fat 15g	**74%**
Cholesterol 195mg	**64%**
Sodium 750mg	**31%**
Total Carbohydrate 14g	**5%**
Dietary Fiber 3g	**12%**
Sugars 6g	
Protein 68g	

Broiled Opah with Toscano Kale

Makes 4 servings   *Kevin Tate*

This recipe makes use of Toscano (Tuscan) kale, also called dino or dinosaur or Lacinato kale, a variety with dark green, slim ruffled leaves and a sweet flavor. This variety grows like a weed in the Islands. Be sure not to overcook the kale; it should have a slight crispness. Butter instead of oil gives this broiled fish dish its touch of the South. Six to 8 cups might sound like a lot of kale, but the vegetable reduces a great deal when cooked, like spinach. Find Toscano kale at Whole Foods, Kokua Market and other health food stores and farmers markets.

2 T.	butter, divided use	6-8 c.	chopped Toscano kale (1 large bunch)
	Juice of ½ lemon		
1 T.	white wine	½ c.	sweet peppers, red, yellow, or orange, short julienne
1½ T.	garlic powder		
½ tsp.	salt	2 T.	extra virgin olive oil
1 T.	fresh thyme, leaves stripped and chopped fine*	1	red onion, sliced thin
		½ tsp.	pepper
1 lb.	opah		

1. Melt butter in microwave (45 seconds at 30 percent). In a zippered plastic bag, combine melted butter, lemon juice, wine, 1 T. garlic powder, ¼ tsp. salt and thyme.
2. Cut fish into 4 even pieces and place in the plastic bag with butter-lemon-thyme marinade; marinate 10 minutes.
3. Broil fish 3 minutes (do not turn). Remove from oven and let sit while preparing kale.
4. Place olive oil in large skillet or wok, heat over medium heat, add onion and peppers and toss to coat with oil.
5. Add kale, remaining garlic powder, salt and pepper. Stir-fry 3 minutes until kale begins to wilt.
6. Add remaining butter. When butter has melted, remove greens to serving plates and top with broiled fish.

To easily strip leaves from stalks of thyme, run fingers down stalk from top to bottom; leaves will pop off.

Nutrition Facts	
Serving Size (298g)	
Servings Per Container	
Amount Per Serving	
Calories 370 Calories from Fat 200	
	% Daily Value*
Total Fat 22g	**33%**
Saturated Fat 7g	**36%**
Cholesterol 75mg	**25%**
Sodium 320mg	**13%**
Total Carbohydrate 19g	**6%**
Dietary Fiber 4g	**15%**
Sugars 2g	
Protein 29g	

Nori, Rice Paper and Shiso-Wrapped Opah with Kabocha-Ginger Puree

Makes 4 servings   *Alan Tsuchiyama*

Opah is what fishermen call a "bi-catch," a species of fish incidentally caught, in this case while long-lining for tuna or swordfish. It is said that, in his early years, Kapi'olani Community College chef instructor Eddie Fernandez was the first chef to prepare and feature opah in the restaurant where he then worked. At that time, mahimahi and the snappers were the only fish most restaurants served.

2 tsp.	shoyu	4 pieces	shiso leaves (perilla, Japanese herb)
1 tsp.	sugar	4 sheets	nori (rolled black seaweed)
½ tsp.	sesame oil		Room-temperature water as needed
⅛ tsp.	sansho (Japanese pepper powder)	4 pieces	rice paper
4 pieces	opah back, (4-5 oz. each)		Rice flour for dredging
1 lb.	kabocha pumpkin, seeded*		Oil for pan frying as needed
1 c.	hot chicken stock		Ume shiso furikake (seaweed
1 T.	grated ginger		condiment) for garnish
¼ tsp.	salt		White pepper to taste

1. In a bowl, mix together the shoyu, sugar, sesame seed oil and sansho.
2. Add the opah and marinate for 1 hour.
3. In a steamer, steam the kabocha until soft. Remove from steamer and cool slightly. When cool enough to handle, remove skin from kabocha and puree through ricer or using a wire whip, until a puree is formed. Add hot chicken stock, ginger, salt and white pepper. Whip until smooth and keep warm for later use. (A good way to do this is to place it in a covered heat-proof bowl in a pot of hot water.)
4. Remove opah from marinade and place a shiso leaf on each piece. Wrap each opah with a nori sheet.
5. Fill a large bowl half-full of room-temperature water. Pass a rice paper wrapper through the water until it is flexible; this happens quickly.
6. Remove the wrapper to a kitchen towel; place another kitchen towel on top to blot.

Nutrition Facts	
Serving Size (262g)	
Servings Per Container	
Amount Per Serving	
Calories 310	Calories from Fat 90
	% Daily Value*
Total Fat 10g	**15%**
Saturated Fat 3g	**15%**
Cholesterol 70mg	**23%**
Sodium 450mg	**19%**
Total Carbohydrate 12g	**4%**
Dietary Fiber 2g	**6%**
Sugars 5g	
Protein 30g	

7. Place one nori wrapped fillet of opah, shiso side down, on softened rice paper. Fold the sides of the rice paper in towards the fish. Then fold the top and bottom sides of the rice paper to enclose the fish with the rice paper.

8. Dredge the packet in rice flour. In a skillet, heat oil and pan-fry opah for about 3 minutes on each side or until medium well-doneness.

9. Serve opah with warm mashed kabocha and sprinkle with ume shiso furikake to add acidity to the dish.

Kabocha, Japanese pumpkin, with its round shape and tough skin, can be a little daunting to cut into. Pop it into the microwave whole for 1 minute and it will cut easily.

Opah Lau Pu'olo (Opah Leaf Packets)

Makes 6 servings   *Corilee Watters and Karl Sloss*

The classical French technique "en papillote," or cooking in parchment packets, is a great way to "steam" fish that have delicate flavors. Encasing the fish in a pre-soaked cedar wrap and ti leaf takes this method to the next level by adding additional moisture and infusing a hint of smokiness. It is reminiscent of the traditional Hawaiian imu-style cooking. We have selected opah here, which is very high in important fatty acids. The tricolors of peppercorns are a colorful reminder of the bright orange-red hues and the thinly sliced oyster mushroom stems of the white dotted skin of the fish. This is a great entrée to serve guests as it can be prepared in advance, requires little monitoring during cooking and is attractive.

6	cedar wraps (6 inch by 6 inch)
1	Meyer lemon, zest and juiced
2 T.	sesame oil
1 T.	mixed peppercorns
2 T.	whole coriander
2 T.	ala'e Hawaiian sea salt
2	ti leaves, large, with mid-ribs removed and each half cut crosswise into 3 sections to yield 12 pieces in total
4 c.	baby bok choy leaves
2 stalks	lemongrass, quartered lengthwise and trimmed to 6-inch length
2 bulbs	shallots, thinly sliced
3 pieces	opah fillets (6 oz. each), cut lengthwise
2 T.	grated fresh young ginger
1 c.	Hāmākua oyster mushroom rondelles
1 c.	bell pepper, red, orange and yellow, julienned
½ cup	fresh cilantro
6 pieces	string to tie 6 wraps, about 8 in. each
3 sheets	parchment paper, cut in halves

Nutrition Facts

Serving Size (185g)
Servings Per Container

Amount Per Serving

Calories 200   Calories from Fat 80

	% Daily Value*
Total Fat 9g	14%
Saturated Fat 2.5g	13%
Cholesterol 55mg	18%
Sodium 620mg	26%
Total Carbohydrate 9g	3%
Dietary Fiber 3g	13%
Sugars 1g	
Protein 23g	

1. Soak cedar wraps and string in water. Zest the lemon rind and squeeze lemon to yield 1 T. of lemon juice, mix with sesame oil, set aside.
2. Grind the peppercorns, coriander seeds and coarse sea salt together with a mortar and pestle, set aside.
3. In the center of each piece of parchment paper, place 1 pre-soaked cedar wrap topped with 1 piece of ti leaf. Next lay down 1-2 bok choy leaves and line with 1 trimmed and quartered lemongrass stalk and shallot slices on top of the bok choy.
4. Season both sides of the fish fillet with the coriander, peppercorn and sea salt spice mix and place fish on top of the shallots lengthwise.
5. Top fish with 1 heaping tablespoon of the grated ginger, lemon juice, lemon zest and sesame oil mixture and spread evenly.
6. Line the top of the fish with oyster mushroom rondelles and the sides with 1-2 julienned strips of red, orange and yellow pepper.
7. Roll the cedar wrap like a sushi roll and tie with soaked string in a double loop. Fold parchment paper around the tied cedar wrap and place in a 9-by-13-inch baking dish.
8. Bake fish packets in baking dish for 18 minutes. Note that cooking time may vary due to ovens and the thickness of the fillet. Use tongs to remove the cedar wrap from the parchment paper and place on a plate.
9. Garnish with fresh cilantro leaves. Serve with rice or noodles.

ʻŌpakapaka
Hawaiʻi Pink Snapper

ʻŌpakapaka, the fishy equivalent of a filet mignon, is too delicious for its own good, with clear, light pink, firm flesh, delicately flavored and much appreciated by the Islands' white tablecloth chefs. This snapper of choice is in danger of being overfished.

Like onaga, ʻōpakapaka is best enjoyed during the winter months and can be prepared in numerous ways. Moderately firm-textured and mild-flavored, it is best with moist heat methods (steaming, braising) but also raw as sashimi. Although ʻōpakapaka contains less EPA, DHA and selenium per serving than onaga, it is still an excellent source of these nutrients. ʻŌpaka-paka is also a good source of vitamins B_3, B_6 and B_{12}.

'Ōpakapaka Provençal

Makes 4 servings   *Eddie Fernandez*

A quick and simple sauce tops grilled 'ōpakapaka fillets, with fragrant jasmine rice to accompany.

4 pieces	'ōpakapaka fillets (9 oz. each)	1 T.	creamy horseradish
	Salt and pepper to taste	4	pitted kalamata olives, sliced into
	All-purpose flour, as needed for		quarters
	dredging	1 T.	capers
2 oz.	canola oil	1 tsp.	Tabasco sauce
¼ lb.	unsalted butter	1 T.	Worcestershire sauce
1 T.	garlic, minced	2 oz.	white wine
1 T.	shallots, minced	2 c.	jasmine rice, cooked and hot
4	large plum tomatoes, diced		

1. Season fish fillets with salt and pepper and dust lightly in flour; set aside on a plate. In a sauté pan on medium-high, heat the oil until hot.
2. Carefully arrange fillets in hot pan and sauté until golden brown, about 1 minute per side. Turn only once. Remove fish, place in heat-proof pan, cover loosely with foil tent and place in warm oven.
3. Discard oil and wipe out sauté pan with paper towel. Add the butter, garlic, shallots, tomatoes, horseradish, olives, capers, Tabasco and Worcestershire sauce and cook about 1 minute.
4. Deglaze with wine and reduce until sauce slightly thickens. Season with salt and pepper to taste.
5. To serve, mound rice in center of each plate; place the fish on the rice and spoon sauce over fish.

Nutrition Facts

Serving Size (519g)
Servings Per Container

Amount Per Serving

Calories 860   Calories from Fat 370

	% Daily Value*
Total Fat 41g	**63%**
Saturated Fat 16g	**79%**
Cholesterol 165mg	**54%**
Sodium 610mg	**25%**
Total Carbohydrate 56g	**19%**
Dietary Fiber 2g	**8%**
Sugars 3g	
Protein 63g	

Thai Fish Soup

Makes 4 servings   *Carol Nardello*

Sprightly Thai-style flavors and the richness of coconut milk make this a memorable soup, which can be made with any firm, white-fleshed fish, though 'ōpakapaka is a special treat.

2 T.	canola oil
1	onion, large, chopped
1	Hawaiian chili pepper (nīoi), chopped*
2 T.	cilantro (leaves and stems), coarsely chopped
2 stalks	lemongrass, trimmed and cut diagonally into 1-inch pieces
1	yam or sweet potato, cubed into ½-inch pieces
1 T.	ginger, freshly grated
3 cloves	garlic, minced
3	limes, zested and juiced
2 cans	coconut milk (13.5 oz. can, light is OK)
4 c.	low-sodium chicken broth
2 T.	fish sauce
2	tomatoes, cubed
1 lb.	'ōpakapaka, cubed into ½-inch pieces
2 stalks	green onions, thinly sliced

1. Heat a large pot over medium heat. Add oil and sauté onions, chili peppers, cilantro, lemongrass, yams, ginger, garlic, lime zest and juice. Stir often, cooking until vegetables are slightly softened, about 5 minutes.
2. Add the coconut milk, broth and fish sauce and bring to a boil. Reduce heat to low and simmer for 15-20 minutes.
3. Add the tomato, 'ōpakapaka and green onions and cook for another 5-8 minutes or until fish is just cooked through.
4. Remove the lemongrass and serve hot.

* Substitute a single tiny hot pepper in place of the Hawaiian chili pepper (nīoi) or use ¼ tsp. cayenne pepper instead.

Nutrition Facts		
Serving Size (389g)		
Servings Per Container		
Amount Per Serving		
Calories 340	Calories from Fat 230	
		% Daily Value*
Total Fat 25g		39%
Saturated Fat 19g		93%
Cholesterol 25mg		8%
Sodium 440mg		18%
Total Carbohydrate 16g		5%
Dietary Fiber 3g		13%
Sugars 3g		
Protein 18g		

Creamy Cajun Fish Stew

Makes 4 servings   *Kevin Tate*

A chowder with a difference, this recipe from Chef Kevin Tate employs 'ōpakapaka, but any similar fish can be substituted. The secret of the flavor is the Cajun Spice, another standard ingredient in Tate's "Southern Fusion" cooking. Almond milk substitutes for more fat-rich dairy products. With almond milk, this recipe is nonfat and gluten-free.

1 T.	extra virgin olive oil
¼ c.	Trinity (celery, onion and red-yellow-orange bell peppers, minced and mixed together)
1 lb.	'ōpakapaka, cut into cubes
1	large red potato, unpeeled, cut into medium dice
2 T.	butter
1 T.	flour
2 c.	unflavored almond milk (or milk or half-and-half)
1 T. + 1 tsp.	Cajun Spice (recipe follows)
¼ tsp.	salt
	Sliced green onion for garnish

1. Heat nonstick skillet over medium-high heat. Add olive oil and Trinity. Toss to coat.
2. Add fish and potato and stir-fry for about 2-3 minutes. Remove fish mixture from skillet and set aside.
3. Return skillet to heat and add butter. Once butter has melted, add flour and whisk until smooth. Gradually add half-and-half or almond milk and whisk until creamy and smooth.
4. Return fish and potato to pan and season with Cajun Spice and salt to taste. Cook until potatoes are softened.
5. Serve hot in bowls with green onion garnish.

Cajun Spice:

½ tsp. garlic powder	½ tsp. oregano
½ tsp. onion powder	¼ tsp. cayenne
½ tsp. paprika	¼ tsp. black pepper
½ tsp. thyme	

Blend and use as desired. (Recipe may be doubled; store in airtight container.)

Nutrition Facts

Serving Size (331g)
Servings Per Container

Amount Per Serving

Calories 340   Calories from Fat 110

	% Daily Value*
Total Fat 12g	**19%**
Saturated Fat 5g	**26%**
Cholesterol 65mg	**22%**
Sodium 440mg	**18%**
Total Carbohydrate 29g	**10%**
Dietary Fiber 2g	**8%**
Sugars 8g	
Protein 30g	

Quenelles of Island Fish

Makes 6 servings   *Wanda A. Adams*

Delicate, egg-shaped pillows of creamed fish called quenelles—or, among our Jewish brethren, gefilte fish—are a wonderfully indulgent way to enjoy 'ōpakapaka or other white-fleshed fish. The fish are poached in a fumet (pronounced "foo-may"), a light stock made from fish bones. If you aren't buying fish whole, ask the fishmonger to sell you some fish heads and bones. Or doctor bottled clam broth with white wine and herbs to get a good-tasting broth. The quenelles are poached in this stock. Though they're great just as they are, the French tradition is to serve these with a rich crayfish or lobster sauce. Our more healthful choice is to serve the quenelles in broth.

For the broth:

	Bones, skin and head from 1-2 fish
2	medium onions, cut into quarters
2	carrots, peeled and cut into chunks
1 tsp.	sea salt
¼ tsp.	white pepper

For the quenelles:

1	sweet (Maui) onion, finely chopped
1 T.	butter
2 lbs.	'opakapaka, cut into cubes*
1	egg
¼ c.	cold water, milk, half-and-half or crème fraîche
1½ tsp.	very fine dry breadcrumbs
½ tsp.	salt
⅛ tsp.	pepper

can also use mahimahi, monchong or a mixture of these fish with butterfish or other more oily but mild-tasting fish

Nutrition Facts	
Serving Size (249g)	
Servings Per Container	
Amount Per Serving	
Calories 220 Calories from Fat 40	
	% Daily Value*
Total Fat 4.5g	**7%**
Saturated Fat 1.5g	**8%**
Cholesterol 100mg	**34%**
Sodium 620mg	**26%**
Total Carbohydrate 9g	**3%**
Dietary Fiber 1g	**6%**
Sugars 4g	
Protein 36g	

Make the broth:

In a large pot of water, combine bones, skin and head, quartered onions, carrot chunks and salt and pepper and bring to a boil. Simmer 10 minutes, taste and correct seasoning. Set aside.

Make the quenelles:

1. Sauté chopped onion in butter. Combine onions, fish, egg, water or half-and-half, crumbs, salt and pepper in food processor and pulse on and off to grind until minced.
2. Dip hands in cold water or use two wet spoons and shape egg-like quenelles. Set aside on a plate.
3. Bring broth to a simmer and gently lower quenelles into simmering broth; cover and simmer gently 45 minutes.
4. Remove quenelles with a slotted spoon and place in shallow warmed bowls. Strain broth and pour gently over quenelles.

Note: You might want to cook one quenelle quickly in the microwave to check seasonings.
Go easy with the salt.

Shutome
Broadbill Swordfish

S hutome, also known as mekajiki, is considered to be the only true species of swordfish. Its flesh typically varies from white to light pink in color and has a long shelf life when handled properly. Shutome is considered the king of billfish, both for the sport it offers and for its mild and moist oily flesh.

Although shutome can be used to make delicious sashimi, it is arguably best used for grilling, smoking and sautéeing. When cooked, the flesh

becomes firm and possesses a rich, hearty flavor. Shutome is extremely rich in EPA and DHA and is also a good source of selenium and vitamins B_3, B_6 and B_{12}.

Grilled Shiso-Marinated Shutome on Wilted Okinawan Spinach

Makes 4 servings   *Alan Tsuchiyama*

Chef Alan Tsuchiyama's first taste of this ultimate swordfish was in Chicago, of all places, where he worked at the world-renowned Drake Hotel, in the Cape Cod Room. He was hooked from that day on. Shiso (perilla, beefsteak plant) is an herb with a delicate, notched leaf; its flavors range from cinnamon to anise in a range of colors from green to purple. Find it at Japanese food stores or farmers markets. Sansho is a Japanese pepper related to the Chinese sichuan pepper. It can be substituted with ground sichuan pepper found in markets in Honolulu's Chinatown. Okinawan spinach is a sturdy green leaf that grows on a bush and thrives in the Islands. The flavor is very green and vegetal. Find it at the Nalo Farms booth at the KCC Farmers Market.

1 stalk	green onion, sliced thinly at a severe angle	1 T.	lemon juice
1 c.	ice water	2 tsp.	sesame oil
8 pieces	shiso leaves, chopped	4 pieces	shutome / broadbill swordfish (4-5 oz. each)
2 tsp.	red miso	1 T.	oil
1 tsp.	sansho (Japanese ground pepper)	1 T.	dried shrimps, chopped
1 tsp.	shichimi togarashi (7-ingredient Japanese chili pepper)	4 oz.	Okinawan spinach
		1 tsp.	black sesame seeds

1. Place sliced green onions in ice water and reserve for later use. In a bowl, mix the shiso, miso, sansho, shichimi togarashi, lemon juice and sesame oil.
2. Place shutome in this marinade and let stand 2 hours or overnight. Drain off excess marinade and place on hot grill.
3. Grill until medium doneness. In a frying pan, heat oil and sauté dried shrimp until shrimp starts to bubble.
4. Add Okinawan spinach and cook until wilted.
5. Arrange spinach on serving plates and arrange shutome over. Drain ice water from green onions and pat dry.
6. Garnish grilled shutome with black sesame seeds and green onion.

Nutrition Facts

Serving Size (233g)
Servings Per Container

Amount Per Serving

Calories 260   Calories from Fat 150

	% Daily Value*
Total Fat 17g	**26%**
Saturated Fat 3.5g	**18%**
Cholesterol 70mg	**23%**
Sodium 250mg	**10%**
Total Carbohydrate 3g	**1%**
Dietary Fiber 1g	**5%**
Sugars 1g	
Protein 26g	

Seafood Miso Soup with Dipping Sauce

Makes 4 servings   *Sharon Kobayashi*

By adding seafood to the broth in this miso soup, and making a tasty dipping sauce, we can cut down on the salt (and eliminate MSG). Use a firm-textured fish or it may fall apart in the soup. Konbu is kelp, which comes in flat, black squares and is quite salty so must be wiped with a damp cloth before use.

2 pieces	dashi konbu (4-by-4-inch squares)	¼ c.	sake
1 slice	ginger, crushed (about 1-inch piece)	3 T.	miso
6 c.	water	4 tsp.	shoyu
½ c.	bonito flakes (2 individual packets)	¼ c.	daikon radish, grated fine
½ lb.	clams (or mussels, scrubbed)		(use a ginger grater for best results)
8	large shrimp	4 tsp.	lemon juice or ponzu
12 oz.	shutome fillet, cut into 1-inch pieces		Steamed baby bok choy or Shanghai
	(substitute opah or mahimahi)		cabbage, sliced green onions (opt.)

1. In a pot, bring konbu, ginger and water to a boil. Remove from heat, add bonito and cover the pot. Let steep at least 15 minutes, strain and discard konbu and bonito. Reserve 2 tablespoons of the broth for the dipping sauce.
2. Bring the rest of the broth to a boil and add clams and shrimp. As soon as clams begin to open and shrimp starts to turn opaque (about 2 minutes), remove from heat and add fish. Mix sake with miso, adding 1 T. of sake at a time till smooth. Add to the broth. Cover and rest 5 minutes or till fish is cooked through.
3. Meanwhile, prepare dipping sauce. In a mixing bowl, combine reserved broth, shoyu, daikon and lemon juice or ponzu.
4. Divide sauce into 4 small bowls or deep saucers (about 2 tablespoons each). Gently re-heat soup (do not bring to a boil).
5. Top each portion with baby bok choy and sliced green onions (if using).
6. Serve with brown rice on the side. Dip fish in sauce as you eat.

Nutrition Facts

Serving Size (556g)
Servings Per Container

Amount Per Serving

Calories 230   Calories from Fat 80

	% Daily Value*
Total Fat 8g	13%
Saturated Fat 2g	11%
Cholesterol 85mg	29%
Sodium 920mg	38%
Total Carbohydrate 7g	2%
Dietary Fiber less than 1g	3%
Sugars 1g	
Protein 29g	

Broiled Swordfish Teriyaki

Makes 4 servings   *Carol Nardello*

Firm-textured swordfish readily stands up to the grill, not breaking up like some flakier varieties.

⅓ c.	low-salt shoyu
3	½-inch slices ginger, smashed
1 T.	sugar
2 cloves	garlic, minced
1 T.	mirin
4 pieces	swordfish steaks (4 oz. or so each)

1. In a small saucepan over medium heat, mix the shoyu, ginger, sugar, garlic and mirin together. Bring to a boil and stir to dissolve the sugar. Remove teriyaki sauce from heat and cool.
2. Carefully arrange the swordfish steaks into a large zippered plastic bag. Pour cooled teriyaki on top and marinate for 2 hours in the refrigerator. Drain the swordfish, reserving the marinade.
3. Pour reserved marinade into a small saucepan. Bring to a boil and reduce to one half. Preheat broiler on high heat.
4. Place fish on the oiled rack of a broiler pan. Brush the fish with reduced marinade and broil 4 inches from the heat for 3 minutes. Carefully, turn fish over and brush again with marinade.
5. Broil 2-3 minutes more until fish is cooked to preferred doneness. Avoid overcooking.

Note: Instead of broiling, grilling 6 inches over hot coals also brings a delicious result.

Nutrition Facts

Serving Size (147g)
Servings Per Container

Amount Per Serving

Calories 200   Calories from Fat 80

	% Daily Value*
Total Fat 9g	**14%**
Saturated Fat 2.5g	**13%**
Cholesterol 60mg	**20%**
Sodium 610mg	**25%**
Total Carbohydrate 7g	**2%**
Dietary Fiber 0g	**0%**
Sugars 4g	
Protein 23g	

Dad's Barbecued Fish

Makes 4 servings

Another use for shutome is a favorite recipe of chef Carol Nardello's father. It can be made with swordfish, as he prefers it, but mahimahi can substitute. You can also use Lawry's Seasoned Salt instead of plain Hawaiian salt for a spicier result. It doesn't get any easier than this.

1 lb.	swordfish fillets or steaks
¼ c.	mayonnaise
1 tsp.	Hawaiian salt or Lawry's Seasoned Salt

1. Preheat grill or broiler on high. Arrange fish on a platter. Coat each piece liberally with mayonnaise. Season with Lawry's. Turn over and repeat.
2. Place coated fish on oiled grill or broiler pan 4-6 inches from heat. Cook for 3-4 minutes.
3. Flip over and cook the other side for 2-3 minutes more or to desired doneness. Avoid overcooking.

Nutrition Facts

Serving Size (128g)
Servings Per Container

Amount Per Serving

Calories 220   Calories from Fat 100

	% Daily Value*
Total Fat 12g	**18%**
Saturated Fat 1.5g	**8%**
Cholesterol 40mg	**13%**
Sodium 470mg	**20%**
Total Carbohydrate 0g	**0%**
Dietary Fiber 0g	**0%**
Sugars 0g	
Protein 29g	

Swordfish Tagine with Chermoula Sauce

Makes 4 servings   *Magdy El-Zoheiry*

This dish is quintessentially North African. A tagine is an earthenware cooking vessel consisting of a shallow round pan for the ingredients and a conical top that directs all the moisture produced during cooking back down into the food. Chermoula is a marinade of herbs, salted lemons and other flavorings. The treatment transforms sometimes tough and dry swordfish into a succulent meal.

For the chermoula sauce:		For the tagine:	
1 T.	American (curly) parsley, leaves only	2 lbs.	swordfish (or substitute nairagi), diced into ¾-inch pieces
1 T.	sweet paprika		
1 T.	ground cumin	2	ripe tomatoes, sliced
1 T.	ground coriander	1	lemon, sliced
½ tsp.	ground ginger	1	red bell pepper, sliced
3 cloves	garlic	1	green bell pepper, sliced
2 T.	lemon juice, fresh squeezed	¼ c.	kalamata olives, seeded
½ tsp.	salt	1 c.	fish stock, clam broth or water
½ tsp.	red pepper flakes (optional)	2 T.	Chermoula Sauce (recipe above)
¼ c.	extra virgin olive oil		

1. Make chermoula sauce: In a food processor or blender, combine all ingredients except olive oil. Process briefly, then begin to drizzle olive oil very slowly through the feed tube until emulsified.
2. Prepare the fish: Pre-heat oven to 400°F. Wash fish under running water, then dry well with a paper towel. Place into tagine dish, Dutch oven or large, deep, oven-proof pan with lid.
3. Add chermoula sauce to the fish, then the tomatoes, lemon, bell peppers, olives and fish stock. Mix all ingredients well. Cover and bake for 20-25 minutes or until the fish is cooked.
4. Drizzle with hot chermoula sauce to serve.

Nutrition Facts

Serving Size (491g)
Servings Per Container

Amount Per Serving

Calories 560   Calories from Fat 340

	% Daily Value*
Total Fat 38g	**58**%
Saturated Fat 8g	**38**%
Cholesterol 120mg	**40**%
Sodium 810mg	**34**%
Total Carbohydrate 14g	**5**%
Dietary Fiber 5g	**22**%
Sugars 4g	
Protein 46g	

Polpette di Shutome e Tombo
(Quenelles of Swordfish and Albacore Tuna)

Makes 4 servings   *Dr. Stephen Bradley*

Here's an unusual recipe for fish balls, formally known as quenelles: ground swordfish and tuna flavored with herbs, Parmesan cheese, lemon and buttery pine nuts and served in a quick, fresh tomato sauce. San Marzano tomatoes are the most highly prized canned tomatoes among knowledgeable lovers of Italian food.

For the fish:

1 lb.	shutome
6 T.	olive oil, divided use
½ lb.	tombo (albacore tuna)
2 oz.	pine nuts
1 tsp.	ground cinnamon
1 tsp.	salt and black pepper
1 tsp.	dried oregano
3 T.	chopped flat-leaf parsley
¼ c.	panko (Japanese dried breadcrumbs)

2 oz.	freshly grated Parmigiano cheese
2	eggs
	Juice and zest of 1 lemon
6 T.	extra virgin olive oil, divided use

For the sauce:

4 cloves	garlic, minced
2 bulbs	shallots, chopped
1 (28-oz.)	can San Marzano tomatoes
1 tsp.	dried oregano

1. Cut the fish into small (¼-in.) dice. In a skillet, heat 3 tablespoons olive oil. Sauté the fish, pine nuts, cinnamon, salt and pepper. Cook until the pine nuts are golden and the fish is cooked through. Set aside in a deep bowl and allow to cool slightly.
2. To this, add the oregano, parsley, panko, Parmigiano cheese, eggs, lemon juice and zest. Fold together gently until well-combined and form into balls or football-shaped ovals using hands or two serving spoons.
3. Place in the refrigerator to rest for about 1 hour.
4. While the polpette are resting, prepare the sauce by cooking the garlic and shallots in remaining olive oil over medium heat until translucent.
5. Tear the tomatoes apart with your hands and add oregano, salt and pepper and cook for about 15 minutes.
6. Place in a food processor or blender and process until smooth.
7. Remove the polpette from the refrigerator and brown in the original skillet.
8. Plate fish balls and top with sauce and chopped parsley.

Nutrition Facts

Serving Size (495g)
Servings Per Container

Amount Per Serving

Calories 690   Calories from Fat 430

	% Daily Value*
Total Fat 48g	**73%**
Saturated Fat 10g	**50%**
Cholesterol 200mg	**67%**
Sodium 650mg	**27%**
Total Carbohydrate 21g	**7%**
Dietary Fiber 5g	**18%**
Sugars 6g	
Protein 50g	

Asian Grilled Broadbill

Makes 4 servings

Eddie Fernandez

Citrus and mustard join familiar Asian flavors, ginger and garlic for this marinated and grilled shutome special.

7 tsp.	shoyu
¼ c.	canola oil
	Zest and juice of 2 lemons
	Zest and juice of 1 orange
2 T.	ginger, minced
2 T.	garlic, minced
2 T.	Dijon mustard
4 pieces	broadbill steaks (6-8 oz. each)
¼ c.	green onions, white parts removed, chopped
4 oz.	sugar snap peas, stem parts removed
2 tsp.	unsalted butter, softened
	Ground black pepper as needed

1. In a small mixing bowl, combine the shoyu, oil, lemon zest, lemon juice, orange zest, orange juice, ginger, garlic and mustard, and mix well with wire whisk.
2. Place broadbill in a single layer into a baking dish. Pour soy-citrus marinade over, cover and refrigerate overnight.
3. Heat grill and brush with a little canola oil to prevent sticking. Remove fish from marinade and season with salt and pepper.
4. Place over hot grill or in oven with broiler setting. Cook until no longer pink in the center, about 10-12 minutes depending on fish thickness.
5. For the sugar snap peas: heat a large skillet until hot. Add the butter and cook until just brown. Add the peas and season with salt and pepper. Cook for about 30 seconds.
6. Place peas in the center of each of 4 plates; arrange the broadbill on top and garnish with green onions.

Nutrition Facts

Serving Size (372g)
Servings Per Container

Amount Per Serving

Calories 520   Calories from Fat 300

	% Daily Value*
Total Fat 33g	**51%**
Saturated Fat 7g	**33%**
Cholesterol 110mg	**37%**
Sodium 880mg	**37%**
Total Carbohydrate 19g	**6%**
Dietary Fiber 6g	**23%**
Sugars 2g	
Protein 41g	

Tombo
Albacore Tuna

Tombo, a.k.a. albacore or white meat tuna, is less oily and rich than its cousins, the yellowfin and big-eye tuna. Though it's most commonly called by its Japanese or English names, it is also known as 'ahipalaha in the Hawaiian language.

Unlike other species of tuna, tombo is best eaten when it is young rather than when it is mature. As a young fish, it is richest in both flavor and omega-3 fatty acids. Tombo has the lightest flavor of Hawai'i's tunas and is often used to prepare sashimi but can be used in any tuna recipe. It is softer textured for tataki, tempura, broiled, baked or smoked. Tombo has the highest amount of EPA and DHA of Hawai'i's tuna varieties and is an excellent source of selenium, magnesium and the vitamins B3, B6 and B12.

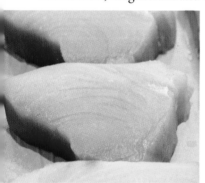

Tombo is sometimes called white tuna due to its light pinkish flesh. Tombo means "dragonfly" in Japanese—it's named for its long pectoral fins. It is a lesser-known species of tuna but is very delicious and usually costs less than 'ahi.

Tuna Niçoise Sandwich

Makes 1 cup serving   *Sharon Kobayashi*

Sweet snow peas, rich olives and tangy Dijon vinaigrette add a delicious and surprising twist to this classic, transformed from a salad to a sandwich for a special-occasion lunch. However, it's easy enough to do any day of the week.

12 oz.	tombo fillet, all in one piece	1 tsp.	salt
2	eggs	½ tsp.	pepper
4 oz.	snow peas, washed, strings removed and cut in half	12	Niçoise olives, seeded and chopped (substitute kalamata)
1 tsp.	shallot, minced	1	large tomato, chopped
2 tsp.	Dijon mustard	2 tsp.	fresh chopped parsley
1 tsp.	Worcestershire sauce	¼ c.	sweet onion, sliced thin
2 tsp.	lemon juice		(Ewa sweet or Maui)
3 tsp.	extra virgin olive oil	1	long baguette, sliced in half

1. Wash eggs thoroughly. Place eggs in a pot of water and bring to a rolling boil. Turn off heat, set timer to 10 minutes, add tuna and cover pot. In the last 2 minutes, add peas and cover again.
2. Meanwhile, make the dressing by combining shallot, mustard, Worcestershire, lemon, oil, salt, pepper and olives.
3. Drain eggs, fish and peas into a colander. When cool enough to handle, peel and chop eggs and flake tuna. Add eggs, tuna and peas to dressing.
4. Add tomatoes, parsley and onion, and toss to combine.
5. Hollow out baguette enough to hold the salad (the removed bread makes great breadcrumbs—freeze for later use).
6. Fill baguette with salad and cut into 4 pieces.
7. If desired, wrap and weight sandwich for 2 hours (refrigerated) before cutting to make it easier to eat.

Note: Ono or aku may be substituted.

Nutrition Facts

Serving Size (242g)
Servings Per Container

Amount Per Serving

Calories 350   Calories from Fat 170

% Daily Value*

Total Fat 19g	**29**%
Saturated Fat 3.5g	**18**%
Cholesterol 140mg	**47**%
Sodium 980mg	**41**%
Total Carbohydrate 15g	**5**%
Dietary Fiber 2g	**9**%
Sugars 4g	
Protein 29g	

Cold Stuffed Artichoke-Tuna Salad

Makes 4 servings   *Sharon Kobayashi*

This is a refreshing lunch or light dinner on a hot summer day when artichokes are in season. Gentle poaching keeps lean fish moist and moderates strong flavors.

4	jumbo artichokes	¼ c.	reduced-fat mayonnaise
2	large eggs	¼ c.	low-fat Greek yogurt
½ lb.	tombo fillet , cut into 2 equal pieces	1½ tsp.	capers, drained and minced
1 clove	garlic, minced	1 tsp.	sea salt
1 tsp.	shallot, minced	½ tsp.	pepper
1 tsp.	Dijon mustard		
1 T.	lemon juice and zest from 1 lemon (plus extra for cooking artichoke)		

Optional for garnish: diced tomato, 1 T. chopped mixed (soft) herbs such as parsley, tarragon or chervil

1. Cut top ⅓ off artichokes and discard. Cut stems off artichokes so artichokes will sit flat when upright. Put artichokes and stems in a pot of water with a dash of lemon juice. Bring to a boil and reduce to a simmer. Cook for approx. 20 minutes or till easily pierced with a knife. Drain and cool upside down.
2. Open (like a flower) and use a spoon to scrape the choke (inedible fibrous hairs) from middle of each artichoke. Discard choke.
3. Peel artichoke stems and dice small. Refrigerate till ready to use. Wrap and refrigerate artichokes till ready to use (this can be done the day before).
4. Add well-washed eggs to a pot of water and bring to a rolling boil. As soon as water boils, add fish, turn off heat, cover and set timer for 10 minutes.
5. At 10 minutes, immediately strain and let cool. Flake fish, peel and chop eggs.
6. Make dressing by combining rest of ingredients.
7. Mix fish, egg and artichoke stems into dressing.
8. When ready to serve, fill the center of each artichoke with fish salad. Top with a little diced tomato and herbs if using.

Note: Papio or aku may be substituted.

Nutrition Facts

Serving Size (285g)
Servings Per Container

Amount Per Serving	
Calories 230	Calories from Fat 50

	% Daily Value*
Total Fat 6g	**9%**
Saturated Fat 2g	**10%**
Cholesterol 130mg	**43%**
Sodium 830mg	**34%**
Total Carbohydrate 22g	**7%**
Dietary Fiber 9g	**36%**
Sugars 6g	
Protein 25g	

Middle Eastern Fishcake Sandwiches

Makes 6 servings   *Wanda A. Adams*

We love okazu-style fishcake, especially when it's made with fresh fish and has a rough rustic texture. Here we stuff fishcake into pita along with vegetables and a wonderful lemony sauce for a healthy, unusual lunch or light supper.

For the fishcake:

1 lb.	tombo, minced
2 tsp.	garlic salt
½ tsp.	black pepper
1 T.	fresh garlic, minced
1 tsp.	grated fresh ginger
¾ tsp.	sesame oil
2 oz.	fine, dry breadcrumbs
	oil for frying

For the sandwiches:

6 pieces	pita bread
1	English cucumber, thinly sliced
1	tomato or equivalent halved cherry or grape tomatoes, thinly sliced
	Mesclun greens, if desired

For the dressing:

1½ c.	tahini (sesame butter)
1½ c.	plain yogurt (preferably a full or lowfat but not nonfat yogurt with natural cultures)
1 clove	garlic, minced
½ c.	fresh lemon juice
¼ c.	minced parsley
1 T.	low-sodium shoyu
	Cayenne or hot sauce to taste (optional)

1. Combine all fishcake ingredients in a bowl and fold together lightly with a wooden spoon. Form small patties, about 2½ inches across. Fry until golden and cooked through. Set aside on paper toweling to drain.
2. Make dressing: Combine all dressing ingredients and blend (stir by hand or use blender or mini food processor). Taste and correct seasonings. This makes a lot; refrigerate leftovers— they're great over hot rice or other grains or any salad.
3. For each sandwich, cut the pita in half and stuff each half with a tuna cake, a couple of slices of cucumber, some tomato and greens. Drizzle in some dressing.

Nutrition Facts

Serving Size (370g)
Servings Per Container

Amount Per Serving

Calories 730   Calories from Fat 330

	% Daily Value*
Total Fat 36g	**56%**
Saturated Fat 6g	**30%**
Cholesterol 35mg	**11%**
Sodium 920mg	**38%**
Total Carbohydrate 63g	**21%**
Dietary Fiber 5g	**22%**
Sugars 8g	
Protein 42g	

Insalata di Tonno, Cipolla e Fagioli
(Tombo Tuna, Onion and Cannellini Bean Salad)

Makes 4 servings   *Dr. Stephen Bradley*

This Italian salad makes use of less expensive tombo and supplements the protein in the fish with mild white beans. The tombo is seared: quickly sautéed over high heat so just the outer layer of fish changes color from red to white; the fish is then turned. The center is left pink.

¼ tsp.	sea salt	4	anchovy fillets
¼ tsp.	freshly-ground black pepper	¼ c.	flat-leaf parsley, chopped
1 lb.	tombo	2 cloves	garlic, finely minced
3 T.	extra virgin olive oil		Pinch sea salt
1	Maui onion	1 tsp.	fresh oregano, chopped
2 T.	wine vinegar		(or 1 tsp. dried)
2 tsp.	water	2 (15-oz.)	cans cannellini beans
4	kalamata olives, pitted		

1. Salt and pepper the tombo, place 1 tsp. olive oil in a skillet over medium heat and sear the tuna for about 5 minutes on each side. Remove from heat and reserve.
2. Cut the onion into quarters and very thinly slice.
3. In a small bowl, marinate onion in wine vinegar and water for 15 minutes, mixing occasionally. Chop the olives and anchovies and combine them in another small bowl with the remaining 2 tsp. olive oil, parsley, oregano and minced garlic.
4. Shred the tombo into rough pieces with 2 forks; set aside. In a sieve or colander, wash the cannellini beans in cold running water to remove the starch. Shake to drain or pat with paper towels.
5. Place the beans in a large salad bowl. Add the olive and herb mixture. Drain the onions and add them.
6. Lastly, add the tombo and toss well to combine.
7. Serve with ciabatta bread.

Nutrition Facts

Serving Size (395g)
Servings Per Container

Amount Per Serving

Calories 440   Calories from Fat 130

	% Daily Value*
Total Fat 15g	**23%**
Saturated Fat 2.5g	**13%**
Cholesterol 50mg	**16%**
Sodium 690mg	**29%**
Total Carbohydrate 34g	**11%**
Dietary Fiber 9g	**35%**
Sugars 1g	
Protein 41g	

Seared Coriander Tombo with Fennel, Cucumber and Orange Salad in Citrus Rice Vinaigrette

Makes 4 servings   *Alan Tsuchiyama*

Chef Alan prefers eating tombo raw to medium rare. Kāʻū oranges are grown in Hawaiʻi. This spice rub was used in an American Culinary Federation student competition and was created by one of the team members. Our culinary future in Hawaiʻi is in good hands with this next generation of culinarians.

3 T.	rice vinegar	1	Kāʻū orange, segmented
2 T.	calamansi juice	1	red radish, sliced thin
2 T.	Kāʻū orange juice		Rough-chopped fennel leaves
	Zest of one Kāʻū orange		as needed
1 tsp.	sugar	1½ T.	fresh ground peppercorn mélange*
¼ c.	grapeseed oil	1½ T.	whole coriander seed
	Fresh-ground black pepper to taste	1½ tsp.	whole cumin
¼ tsp.	salt	4 pieces	tombo (4-5 oz. each)
1 bulb	fennel (small bulb), sliced very thin		Olive oil as needed to sauté
4 inches	local Japanese cucumber, skinned, seeded and sliced thin		

1. In a small bowl mix together the rice vinegar, calamansi juice, orange juice, orange zest, sugar, grapeseed oil, pepper and salt. Set aside vinaigrette for the salad.
2. In a bowl, mix the fennel, cucumbers, orange segments, radish and fennel leaves with the vinaigrette.
3. In a spice grinder, mix the peppercorn mélange, coriander seed and cumin and grind. Season tombo with salt and generously coat with the spice mixture.
4. In a skillet heat the olive oil and sauté the tombo until the desired doneness. Chef Alan likes it still raw in the middle— sautéed about 15 seconds on each side.
5. Cool slightly, slice and serve with the fennel salad.

Variation: For an appetizer. the tombo can be cut into sashimi blocks.

*Peppercorn mélange is an assortment of peppercorns mixed together. If you cannot find it, black peppercorns will do.

Nutrition Facts

Serving Size (306g)
Servings Per Container

Amount Per Serving	
Calories 350	Calories from Fat 150

	% Daily Value*
Total Fat 17g	**26%**
Saturated Fat 2.5g	**12%**
Cholesterol 50mg	**17%**
Sodium 270mg	**11%**
Total Carbohydrate 15g	**5%**
Dietary Fiber 5g	**19%**
Sugars 5g	
Protein 37g	

Uku
Blue-Green Snapper

Uku is often the available choice among Hawaiian bottom fish when there's a ban on other species. At such a time, it would be the only fresh Hawaiian snapper on the market because the uku fishery is considered sustainable and not endangered by overfishing. The texture is a bit firmer than that of other snappers, but uku is definitely good eating. Uku are available year round, but unlike onaga and 'opakapaka, summer is the peak season for the harvesting of this fish.

The delicate flavor and moderately firm texture of uku rivals that of its snapper cousins and makes for a great substitute. Take care not to overcook. It's best for sashimi or baked, steamed or sautéed. Uku is a good source of EPA, DHA, selenium and vitamins B_3, B_6 and B_{12}.

Pan-Fried Cornmeal Uku on Potato with Kale and Portuguese Sausage

Makes 4 servings   *Alan Tsuchiyama*

Here, local produce—potatoes and kale—and the Island favorite Portuguese sausage join forces with uku for a flavorful and attractive entree.

2 T.	canola oil	1 T.	fresh Italian parsley, rough chopped
1 lb.	potatoes cut into bite-size pieces	1 T.	lemon juice
1	Maui onion, medium, sliced into strips	¼ tsp.	salt
			ground black pepper to taste
1 T.	garlic, chopped	16 oz.	uku, cut into 2-oz. pieces, sliced thin
1	Portuguese sausage, cut bite size		Flour as needed for dredging
½ tsp.	fresh thyme leaves, rough chopped	2	eggs, beaten
1 tsp.	fresh oregano leaves, rough chopped		Cornmeal as needed for dredging
2 c.	kale, rough chopped		Oil for frying

1. In a skillet, heat canola oil and sauté potatoes on medium heat. Cook until light brown and almost cooked through.
2. Add Maui onions and garlic; cook until onions are translucent.
3. Add Portuguese sausage and cook until well done.
4. Add thyme, oregano and kale and cook until greens are wilted. Add Italian parsley, lemon juice, salt and ground black pepper. Remove from heat.
5. On a flat pan or plate, season uku with salt and pepper. Place flour on a separate plate, beat eggs into small bowl and place cornmeal on another flat plate.
6. Dredge* uku with flour, then coat with beaten eggs and finally dredge in cornmeal. In a skillet, heat the oil. When oil is hot, fry the uku until done. On a plate, place the potato, kale and Portuguese sausage mixture and arrange uku on top.

*To dredge is to coat an item with flour, cornstarch, cornmeal or other bread. Gently drag protein through bedding or press lightly into breading.

Nutrition Facts	
Serving Size (425g)	
Servings Per Container	
Amount Per Serving	
Calories 660 Calories from Fat 290	
	% Daily Value*
Total Fat 32g	49%
Saturated Fat 8g	39%
Cholesterol 215mg	72%
Sodium 800mg	33%
Total Carbohydrate 45g	15%
Dietary Fiber 5g	20%
Sugars 3g	
Protein 47g	

Portuguese Uku Pūpū

Makes 4-6 servings

Wanda A. Adams

Continuing with the Portuguese theme is this classic pūpū, ideal for beer, the back of the truck and pau hana. Back in the day, every local Portuguese home had a nīoi (Hawaiian chili pepper) plant in the yard, producing bright red or yellow explosions of fire and flavor and a few thriving bunches of salsa (flat-leaf parsley). Adjust the amount of chili and garlic to your taste. One of the hallmarks of Portuguese cooking is the use of vinegar to perk up the palate; be sure to cut it a bit with water. Here, marinated uku is broiled; it's also common to quickly braise the fish in the marinade. You can use bone-in pieces, steaks, even the collar (aku bone) or fillets; don't overcook boneless fillets. It's smart to wear kitchen gloves when working with chili pepper; whatever you do, don't touch the eyes, lips or nose with chili juices on your hands.

For the pūpū:

2 lb.	uku steaks, fillets or other pieces*
1	fresh chili pepper, small, seeded and diced
2 tsp.	Hawaiian salt
1-2 cloves	garlic, minced
¾ c.	cider vinegar
¼ c.	water
	Olive oil

For the onion topping:

1 T.	onion, minced, and a few very thinly sliced rounds of onion for garnish
1 T.	parsley, minced
½	fresh chili pepper, small, seeded (optional)
½ tsp.	Hawaiian salt
1½ T.	cider vinegar

Nutrition Facts

Serving Size (213g)
Servings Per Container

Amount Per Serving

Calories 180   Calories from Fat 35

	% Daily Value*
Total Fat 3.5g	**6%**
Saturated Fat 0g	**0%**
Cholesterol 65mg	**22%**
Sodium 670mg	**28%**
Total Carbohydrate 4g	**1%**
Dietary Fiber 0g	**0%**
Sugars 3g	
Protein 32g	

1. Place fish in flat, nonreactive container with cover.
2. In a bowl, stir together chili, salt, vinegar and water, pour over fish and allow to marinate, covered, for at least an hour, turning once.
3. Combine onion topping ingredients in a separate nonreactive bowl and marinate 15 minutes or more.
4. Preheat broiler and brush with olive oil. Broil fish 3-4 minutes, turn and repeat. Place fish in rimmed bowl or platter.
5. Pour sauce over hot fish. Serve with cold beer and crusty country-style bread for dipping up the juices.

This recipe is great with aku, too.

Tip: You can just pick it up with chopsticks, eat it with a spoon, dip in with your hands or spread it on the bread. It's a bit messy but so-o-o-o 'ono.

Fish Curry in Yogurt Sauce

Makes 6 servings   *Kusuma Cooray*

Here, yogurt yields a thick, velvety sauce redolent with the spices of the East. Be sure not to overcook the fish and to handle the fillets gently so they don't break into shreds in the pan. Serve with rice or other grains and a simply cooked vegetable.

6 pieces	uku fillets, 6 oz. each
2 T.	lemon juice
	Sea salt to taste
3 T.	olive oil
1 c.	finely sliced onion
1 c.	finely sliced tomatoes
2	green chilies, seeded and sliced
1 tsp.	peeled, chopped fresh ginger
2 tsp.	curry powder
½ tsp.	paprika
¼ tsp.	turmeric
¼ tsp.	cayenne
1 c.	yogurt
½ c.	water
¼ c.	fresh mint, chopped

1. Season the fish fillets with lemon juice and salt; refrigerate. Heat olive oil in sauté pan and cook onions until golden.
2. Add tomatoes, chilies and ginger; cook 3 minutes. Add spices and cook 3 minutes. Whisk together yogurt and water and stir into sauce.
3. Transfer fish fillets to pan and simmer gently for 3 minutes.
4. Using a spatula, turn the fish and simmer an additional 3 minutes. Taste and season as needed, garnishing with fresh chopped mint.

Nutrition Facts

Serving Size (300g)
Servings Per Container

Amount Per Serving

Calories 300   Calories from Fat 80

% Daily Value*

Total Fat 9g	**14%**
Saturated Fat 1.5g	**7%**
Cholesterol 70mg	**23%**
Sodium 150mg	**6%**
Total Carbohydrate 10g	**3%**
Dietary Fiber 2g	**6%**
Sugars 6g	
Protein 47g	

Furikake Uku

Makes 6 servings   *Carol Nardello*

Preparing this dish is about as easy as it gets—but so delicious with hot rice and a cool Japanese-style cucumber salad. If you want to get a little fancy, go to the chill section of a Japanese grocery and look for small vacuum-packed packages of kirashi wasabi—chopped, fresh wasabi. It's got more of a kick and some texture, too. Many furikake fish recipes are fried, but this one saves some fat by being baked. You can use low-fat mayonnaise. Furikake, by the way, is a Japanese condiment of seeds, strips of seaweed, dried fish, salt and sugar. There are several types; nori kome is perhaps most commonly used.

½ c.	mayonnaise
1 T.	wasabi paste (more or less to taste)
1½ lb.	uku fillets
3 T.	furikake

1. Preheat oven to 375°. Spray a sheet tray or baking pan with cooking spray. In a small bowl, combine mayonnaise and wasabi together. Whisk until smooth.
2. Arrange fish in prepared pan. Spread wasabi-mayo evenly on top of fish. Sprinkle furikake all over coated side of fish.
3. Bake in hot oven for 10-12 minutes or until desired doneness.

Nutrition Facts

Serving Size (138g)
Servings Per Container

Amount Per Serving

Calories 260   Calories from Fat 150

% Daily Value*

Total Fat 16g	**25%**
Saturated Fat 2g	**10%**
Cholesterol 55mg	**19%**
Sodium 260mg	**11%**
Total Carbohydrate 1g	**0%**
Dietary Fiber less than 1g	**2%**
Sugars 1g	
Protein 24g	

PART III

AQUACULTURE SEAFOOD

Butterfish
Black Cod, Sablefish

It is all but impossible to find undressed black cod in the fish section of the average Island grocery store. One dish—misoyaki ("grilled with miso") or misozuke ("marinated in miso") butterfish—is so ubiquitous and popular that it seems to take up the whole catch. You can buy the fish bathed in white miso almost everywhere, but to get plain, fresh black cod you may need the help of a good fish purveyor. Big Island Butterfish is raised by Troutlodge Marine Farms at the Natural Energy Laboratory of Hawai'i in Kona, grown in the icy cold waters pumped up from off the coast. However, this product is sold mostly to restaurants at this time.

Cooking tips: Oil-rich with a buttery flavor, butterfish stands up to more robust cooking methods such as marinating with strong flavoring agents like misoyaki, then broiling or searing. It's good with almost any method of cooking. Butterfish provide a good source of EPA and DHA omega-3s.

Butterfish and Watermelon Salad

Makes 4 servings   *Sharon Kobayashi*

This is a refreshing salad to serve during the summer, when watermelon is at its best. Be sure the watermelon is sweet and juicy to offset the peppery arugula and buttery black cod. If black cod is unavailable, use another rich, flaky fish such as salmon.

1 lb.	butterfish/black cod, cut into 4-oz. steaks
1 T.	white miso
1 T.	low-sodium shoyu
½ tsp.	sea salt
2 tsp.	vegetable oil
½ c.	balsamic vinegar
4 tsp.	extra virgin olive oil
1 lb.	seedless watermelon
4 c.	baby arugula

1. Marinate the fish in miso, shoyu and salt overnight. Pre-heat a non-stick skillet on medium and add vegetable oil, swirling to coat.
2. Cook fish and marinating liquids about 6 minutes (flipping halfway thorough) or till liquids evaporate and fish is light brown.
3. Meanwhile, prepare plates by arranging watermelon and arugula. Top with fish.
4. Add vinegar to the hot pan. Cook till reduced and thickened, about 2 minutes. Drizzle evenly over each dish.
5. Drizzle each plate with 1 tsp. olive oil and serve immediately.

Nutrition Facts

Serving Size (292g)
Servings Per Container

Amount Per Serving

Calories 370   Calories from Fat 220

	% Daily Value*
Total Fat 24g	**38%**
Saturated Fat 4.5g	**23%**
Cholesterol 55mg	**19%**
Sodium 500mg	**21%**
Total Carbohydrate 24g	**8%**
Dietary Fiber 2g	**8%**
Sugars 20g	
Protein 17g	

Roasted Butterfish with Fennel and Tomato

Makes 4 servings   *Sharon Kobayashi*

Roasted butterfish is ideal for a romantic dinner for two (use a cast iron skillet and halve the recipe). The key to this restaurant-quality recipe is to use very good, fresh fish; ripe, flavorful tomatoes and a young, fruity, drinkable wine (both for the dish and to serve at the table). Fennel is a vegetable with the texture of celery and an anise-like perfume and is readily available in grocery stores.

1 lb.	butterfish, cut into 2 pieces (8-oz. steaks)
1	fennel bulb, medium, cut into 8 sections (plus 1 T. fronds, minced)
2 c.	cherry tomatoes
8	bay leaves, fresh if possible
8 cloves	garlic
1½ tsp.	salt
½ tsp.	black peppercorns, crushed
1 T.	extra virgin olive oil
⅔ c.	red wine (merlot or shiraz/syrah)

1. Preheat oven to 425°. In a roasting pan (preferably non-stick or foil-lined), arrange cod with fennel, tomatoes, bay leaves and garlic scattered on and about the fish.
2. Use 1 tsp. of the salt to rub into both sides of fish steaks, sprinkle the remaining salt and pepper over everything. Sprinkle the oil evenly over the vegetables.
3. Bake for 35 to 40 minutes, or till the liquids evaporate and the fish just begins to brown. Remove fish to a serving plate. Then deglaze the pan: Immediately add the wine to the remaining juices and browned bits, stirring to loosen solids.
4. If mixture does not thicken enough, return to the oven for 5 minutes or till it reaches sauce consistency.
5. Pour mixture over fish and garnish with fennel fronds.

Note: Salmon may be substituted for butterfish.

Nutrition Facts

Serving Size (298g)
Servings Per Container

Amount Per Serving

Calories 320   Calories from Fat 190

	% Daily Value*
Total Fat 21g	**33%**
Saturated Fat 4g	**21%**
Cholesterol 55mg	**19%**
Sodium 970mg	**41%**
Total Carbohydrate 10g	**3%**
Dietary Fiber 3g	**12%**
Sugars 2g	
Protein 17g	

Misoyaki Butterfish

Makes 4 servings   *Sharon Kobayashi*

You can't have a butterfish section in an Island cookbook without a misoyaki butterfish recipe. Though you can buy butterfish already marinated, making your own allows you to alter the flavors just as you like. Use a good-quality sake, one that you'd drink at the table. And use a good, fresh, locally made miso. The best tool for grating daikon (white radish or Asian/Japanese radish) and ginger is a saucer-like porcelain oroshigane, with tiny sharp teeth that make short work of shredding the vegetables and a moat around the edge to catch any juices. You can serve the butterfish as is with hot rice, or drizzle it with a hot vinaigrette or a citrus butter for an additional layer of flavor.

1 c.	sake
1 c.	mirin (sweetened rice wine)
1 c.	sugar (may use white, brown or a combination)
4 oz.	fresh white miso (fermented soybean paste)
4 pieces	butterfish fillets (4 oz. each)
1 T.	vegetable oil
	Peeled and grated daikon and ginger for garnish

1. In a saucepan, combine sake, mirin, sugar and miso; cook over medium heat until caramel-colored. Remove from heat, cool and place in zippered plastic bag. Wipe butterfish free of moisture and add to bag.
2. Marinate overnight. Shortly before serving, heat vegetable oil over medium heat.
3. Shaking off excess marinade, place fillets in pan. Do not overcrowd fish.
4. Sauté 4 minutes on each side, until slightly caramelized and golden.
5. Serve with finely grated daikon and ginger as a garnish.

Nutrition Facts

Serving Size (313g)
Servings Per Container

Amount Per Serving

Calories 650   Calories from Fat 110

	% Daily Value*
Total Fat 13g	**19**%
Saturated Fat 4g	**21**%
Cholesterol 75mg	**25**%
Sodium 950mg	**40**%
Total Carbohydrate 81g	**27**%
Dietary Fiber 5g	**19**%
Sugars 73g	
Protein 25g	

Island-Raised Shrimp

You have to have a long memory to recall when Oʻahu's North Shore wasn't paved with shrimp shacks. The business has faced many challenges and companies have come and gone, but aquaculture enthusiasts persist, even if some of those shrimp trucks and shrimp shacks are selling previously frozen imported shrimp. How to tell the shack is really engaged in aquaculture? They have live shellfish to sell you. North Shore growers raise both shrimp and the immense, hoary-looking red-whiskered, blue-clawed Tahitian prawns. On Kauaʻi, meanwhile, tender, sweet shrimp are raised in specially designed ponds fed by deep seawater wells. Warm-water shrimp like the species raised in Hawaiʻi are generally considered the best flavored.

Shrimp turns rubbery and loses much of its rich flavor when overcooked. Limit the cooking time and allow for carry-over cooking (when the heat retained in the seafood continues to cook the flesh after it's removed from the heat). Shrimp contains some EPA and DHA, as well as zinc, selenium and vitamins A, B_3, B_5 and B_{12}.

Spicy Baked Shrimp

Makes 6 servings   *Carol Nardello*

What could be easier than serving a dish that marinates and bakes in the same pan? This makes for a great pūpū when served in a lettuce wrap. Just spoon some of the prepared shrimp onto a small chilled lettuce leaf, roll or fold, and enjoy. Also serves as a simple entrée over rice or egg noodles.

¼ c.	vegetable oil
3 T.	Southwest Seasoning (recipe follows)
3 T.	lemon juice
3 T.	parsley, chopped
1½ T.	sugar
1 T.	low-sodium shoyu
⅛ tsp.	cayenne pepper
4 cloves	garlic, minced
2 lb.	uncooked shrimp, large, peeled and deveined

1. In a medium bowl, combine oil, seasoning, lemon juice, parsley, sugar, shoyu, cayenne and garlic. Whisk to blend well. Add shrimp and toss to coat evenly. Place shrimp in a 9-by-13-inch pan to marinate. Seal tightly. Refrigerate overnight.
2. Preheat oven to 400°. Place pan filled with shrimp and marinade into the hot oven. Bake, stirring once or twice, for about 12 minutes or until done. Delicious served over hot rice. Allow extra time to bake when preparing jumbo-sized shrimp.

Southwest Seasoning

5 T.	paprika
2 T.	onion powder
4 T.	garlic powder
2 T.	cayenne pepper
½ T.	sea salt
2 T.	oregano
2 T.	black pepper
2 T.	thyme

Mix together and store in a tightly sealed container.

Nutrition Facts

Serving Size (139g)
Servings Per Container

Amount Per Serving	
Calories 210	Calories from Fat 80

	% Daily Value*
Total Fat 9g	14%
Saturated Fat 1g	6%
Cholesterol 170mg	57%
Sodium 750mg	31%
Total Carbohydrate 7g	2%
Dietary Fiber 1g	5%
Sugars 3g	
Protein 24g	

Shrimp Appetizer

Makes 10-12 appetizer servings   *Carol Nardello*

Need an easy cold pūpū that you can prepare early in the day? Try this one. So quick, and sure to please!

1 pkg.	cream cheese (16 oz.), at room temperature
1 T.	Old Bay Seasoning (recipe follows)
1	lime, zested and juiced
8 dashes	Tabasco sauce
1 tsp.	salt
½ tsp.	white pepper
1 loaf	crusty baguette, sliced into rounds
2 lb.	shrimp, medium size, cooked and chilled
½ c.	flat-leaf parsley, chopped

1. In a medium mixing bowl, with an electric mixer, combine the cream cheese, Old Bay Seasoning, lime zest and juice, Tabasco, salt and pepper. Mix until smooth and creamy.
2. Put cheese mixture into a large pastry bag with a medium star tip. Pipe a generous tablespoonful of cheese onto each bread slice.
3. Top with 1 or more shrimp. Garnish with parsley. Chill well before serving.

Old Bay Seasoning

1 T.	ground bay leaves
½ tsp.	white pepper
2 tsp.	celery salt
½ tsp.	nutmeg
1½ tsp.	dry mustard
½ tsp.	ginger
1 tsp.	black pepper
½ tsp.	allspice
1 tsp.	paprika
¼ tsp.	ground cloves
½ tsp.	celery seeds
¼ tsp.	cayenne pepper

Mix together and store tightly sealed. Keeps for weeks.

Nutrition Facts

Serving Size (152g)
Servings Per Container

Amount Per Serving

Calories 280   Calories from Fat 160

% Daily Value*

Total Fat 18g	**28%**
Saturated Fat 10g	**52%**
Cholesterol 190mg	**63%**
Sodium 660mg	**27%**
Total Carbohydrate 6g	**2%**
Dietary Fiber less than 1g	**3%**
Sugars 0g	
Protein 22g	

Kauaʻi Shrimp Cake with Papaya and Ginger Salsa

Makes 6 cakes   *Sharon Kobayashi*

Most types of shrimp are very firm when cooked, but Kauaʻi shrimp has a soft texture that is ideal in this crab cake-type recipe. It is best very fresh, so check with the stores (fish markets, Times Super-markets and Costco) to see when it comes in and use it right away.

2 lbs.	fresh Kauaʻi shrimp (substitute 1 lb. crab meat)	2 tsp.	yellow mustard
		1 tsp.	sriracha hot sauce
2 T.	onion, minced	¼ c.	egg substitute*
2 cloves	garlic, minced	1 c.	panko bread crumbs, divided use
2 T.	Thai basil, minced	4 tsp.	vegetable oil
2 stalks	celery, minced	1 recipe	Spicy Papaya and Ginger Salsa
¼ c.	reduced-fat mayonnaise		(recipe follows)

Optional: Serve with micro greens, sunflower sprouts or shredded cabbage

1. Remove heads and peel shrimp (discard or save for stock).
2. Bring a pot of water to a boil, and cook shrimp for 10 seconds or until just opaque. Drain, cool and chop shrimp (pea-size pieces). Transfer to a mixing bowl.
3. Add onion, garlic, basil, celery, mayonnaise, mustard, sriracha, egg and ½ cup panko. Mix gently and form six ½-cup patties. Cover and refrigerate for 1 hour to set.
4. Dredge cakes in remaining ½ cup panko.
5. Pre-heat a heavy-bottom skillet on medium high. Add 2 tsp. of the oil to the pan, coating it evenly. Cook cakes on one side for 5 minutes, or till deep brown. Drizzle remaining oil over cakes, flip over and continue to cook for an additional 5 minutes (or till brown).
6. Serve with the salsa and micro greens (if using).

* Use the liquid form found in supermarket chillers.

Nutrition Facts	
Serving Size (283g)	
Servings Per Container	
Amount Per Serving	
Calories 290	Calories from Fat 70
	% Daily Value*
Total Fat 8g	**12%**
Saturated Fat 1.5g	**6%**
Cholesterol 230mg	**77%**
Sodium 580mg	**24%**
Total Carbohydrate 20g	**7%**
Dietary Fiber 2g	**8%**
Sugars 6g	
Protein 34g	

Spicy Papaya and Ginger Salsa

(Makes about 1 cup)

1	papaya, large, diced (firm but ripe)
1 T.	shallot, minced
1 T.	cilantro, minced
½ tsp.	ginger, grated fine

½ tsp.	hot sauce, or to taste
1 tsp.	fish sauce
¼ tsp.	salt
1 tsp.	sugar
2 T.	lime juice

Combine all ingredients; refrigerate for 1 hour.

Shrimp with Mint and Feta

Makes 4 appetizer servings   *Magdy El-Zoheiry*

Could a shrimp dish be easier? You simply grill the shrimp, toss with a few bright-flavored ingredients and serve with pita bread to soak up the juices. Try the pita from Agnes Bakery in Kailua; it doesn't have pockets, but it's made with whole grains and is light and puffy (also available at Down to Earth).

12	shrimp (16-20 per pound), peeled and deveined
1 T.	extra virgin olive oil
1 T.	lime juice
2 T.	feta cheese, crumbled
1 T	fresh mint leaves, chopped
¼ tsp.	salt
	Freshly ground pepper to taste
2 pieces	pita bread, each cut in half

1. Season shrimp with salt and pepper. Grill shrimp until it is cooked, about three minutes on each side.
2. Place grilled shrimp in a mixing bowl and toss with olive oil, feta, mint, pepper and lime juice.
3. Mix well until shrimp is coated and properly seasoned.
4. Serve with pita. Garnish with lime wedges and sprigs of mint.

Nutrition Facts

Serving Size (64g)
Servings Per Container

Amount Per Serving

Calories 150   Calories from Fat 45

% Daily Value*

Total Fat 5g	**8%**
Saturated Fat 1.5g	**7%**
Cholesterol 35mg	**12%**
Sodium 390mg	**16%**
Total Carbohydrate 18g	**6%**
Dietary Fiber less than 1g	**4%**
Sugars 1g	
Protein 8g	

Kahuku Prawn Saganaki (Pan-Fried Greek-Style Prawns)

Makes 6 servings   *Dr. Stephen Bradley*

Saganaki is a Greek term for a cooking style in which a savory dish of chopped or grated ingredients is prepared in a single pan and allowed to melt and brown into a crisp cake. A particular favorite is an appetizer of fried cheese. Saganaki means "little frying pan."

½ c.	extra virgin olive oil
2	onions, medium, finely sliced
2 cloves	garlic, minced
8 oz.	cherry tomatoes, halved
1 tsp.	tomato paste
1 c.	dry white wine
12	large shrimp, cleaned, de-veined, tail intact
6 oz.	feta cheese, crumbled
2 T.	flat-leaf parsley, chopped
2 T.	fresh oregano, chopped
½ tsp.	sea salt
¼ tsp.	freshly ground black pepper
	Crusty bread

1. Preheat the oven to 400°. In an ovenproof skillet, heat the olive oil over medium heat. Add the onions and garlic and sauté until soft, about 5 minutes.
2. Add the tomatoes and tomato paste and cook for another 10 minutes. Add the wine and allow to reduce until mostly absorbed. Add the salt and pepper, followed by the shrimp and oregano. Sauté for 5 more minutes.
3. Sprinkle with feta cheese and bake for an additional 5 minutes to allow the cheese to melt.
4. Sprinkle the chopped parsley and serve immediately with good crusty bread.

Nutrition Facts

Serving Size (162g)
Servings Per Container

Amount Per Serving

Calories 310   Calories from Fat 230

	% Daily Value*
Total Fat 25g	**39**%
Saturated Fat 7g	**35**%
Cholesterol 45mg	**16**%
Sodium 480mg	**20**%
Total Carbohydrate 7g	**2**%
Dietary Fiber less than 1g	**3**%
Sugars 3g	
Protein 8g	

Coconut Shrimp with Mango Sauce

Makes 6 servings   *Carol Nardello*

2 lb.	shrimp, peeled and deveined (jumbo size preferred)
1 c.	panko
1 c.	shredded coconut
4	eggs
½ tsp.	spicy Hawaiian seasoned salt
1 c.	flour
1 tsp.	curry powder
2 tsp.	onion powder
2 tsp.	garlic powder
	Quick Mango Sauce (recipe follows)
2-3 in.	canola or peanut oil in a pot for deep-frying

1. Preheat oil to 350° F.
2. In a medium bowl, combine panko and coconut to make crumb mixture.
3. In a small bowl, mix together eggs and seasoned salt.
4. In a third bowl, combine flour, curry, and onion and garlic powders.
5. Dredge shrimp in seasoned flour.
6. Dip into egg mixture.
7. Coat with crumb mixture.
8. Cook in 3 batches in hot oil for 2-3 minutes or until crisp and golden brown.
9. Drain on paper towels.
10. Serve hot with Quick Mango Sauce.

Quick Mango Sauce

½ c.	sweet chili sauce
1	lime, zested
1	mango, peeled, seeded and diced into ½-in. pieces

1. Combine chili sauce and lime zest. Stir until smooth. Gently fold in diced mangos.
2. Serve with Coconut Shrimp.
3. Refrigerate any leftover sauce.

Nutrition Facts

Serving Size (239g)
Servings Per Container

Amount Per Serving

Calories 440   Calories from Fat 200

	% Daily Value*
Total Fat 22g	**34%**
Saturated Fat 5g	**26%**
Cholesterol 280mg	**93%**
Sodium 500mg	**21%**
Total Carbohydrate 31g	**10%**
Dietary Fiber 3g	**10%**
Sugars 9g	
Protein 29g	

Portuguese Piripiri Shrimp

Makes 6-8 appetizer servings   *Wanda A. Adams*

This recipe ought to have yellow police tape around it: Warning, not for the faint of palate. It's spicy but so-o-o-o addictively delicious and easy for an appetizer. It's known all over Portugal, where they even have special little heat-proof ceramic dishes for serving it. Shrimp is marinated, grilled and bathed in warm olive oil spiked with piripiri, the fiery chili sauce of Portugal. If you don't want to make piripiri, sambal oelek makes a good substitute, or even Chinese garlic chili paste.

2 lb.	large shrimp, peeled and deveined (okay to leave tail on)
1 T.	minced garlic
1 T.	peeled and minced chilies (i.e., Hawaiian red chili, nioi); use less if you're timid
1½ cups	extra virgin olive oil
	Good, crusty, country-style bread, torn, not sliced
	Piripiri sauce or other chili sauce (recipe follows)

1. Place peeled and deveined shrimp in a container with a lid and add minced garlic, chilies and enough olive oil to moisten the contents. Stir and place in refrigerator overnight. Stir occasionally or shake.
2. Shortly before serving, broil or grill shrimp just until they turn pink.
3. Meanwhile, in a saucepan, heat 1 cup extra virgin olive oil. Pour a shallow pool of hot oil into individual ramekins or other heat-proof shallow serving dishes.
4. Place 2 or 3 shrimp in each dish, serve with good bread.
5. Pass the piripiri sauce, which can also be drizzled over the dish.
6. Use as much or as little piripiri as you desire. (You can also add more minced garlic to the hot oil if you like.)

Piripiri Sauce

There are as many recipes for piripiri as there are Portuguese households, but the basic ingredients are always hot red peppers, olive oil and some form of acid. Other hot pepper sauces such as Tabasco or Tapatío just won't taste right. This will keep at room temperature or in the fridge.

4-6	hot red chili peppers (Hawaiian peppers, nioi)
1 tsp.	sea salt
1 c.	olive oil
⅓ c.	cider vinegar or fresh lemon juice

1. Coarsely chop the peppers and place in a sterile jar along with salt, oil and vinegar or lemon juice. Cover tightly, shake and store at room temperature.
2. For a mellower flavor, use Thai red peppers, which aren't as hot.
3. You can also roast the peppers at 300° for 15 minutes for a milder, slightly smoky flavor.

Nutrition Facts

Serving Size (196g)
Servings Per Container

Amount Per Serving

Calories 600   Calories from Fat 410

	% Daily Value*
Total Fat 45g	70%
Saturated Fat 6g	31%
Cholesterol 170mg	57%
Sodium 360mg	15%
Total Carbohydrate 21g	7%
Dietary Fiber 2g	9%
Sugars 2g	
Protein 26g	

Kona Abalone

For a generation, abalone meant canned top shell, a type of marine snail that tastes like abalone. Fresh abalone was a thing of the past. Now, through the efforts of Big Island Abalone Corp., another aquaculture operation located at the NELHA facility in Kona, fresh abalone are again available in Hawai'i. You can find them at the KCC Saturday Farmers Market. They can be mail-ordered (www.bigislandabalone.com) and cooked in retort pouches, too.

A gourmet favorite, abalone comes with a price to match its exquisite flavor. It also requires some tenderizing technique and can overcook very quickly. It's best prepared with one of the simpler cooking methods—top shucked, braised or steamed with sauce—or served as sashimi.

Abalone Sashimi with Lomi Kizami Wasabi and Tomato

Makes 2 appetizer servings   *Alan Tsuchiyama*

Abalone Sashimi is close to Chef Alan's heart and now not quite as far from his wallet. This dish utilizes a prepared kizami wasabi (seasoned stems of the wasabi plant; find it in squeeze tubes in the chill case at Marukai). Or this ingredient can be replaced with a mixture of blanched chopped spinach stems, wasabi paste, mirin and salt. If you aren't using abalone, try opihi, king clam, cooked octopus or that old canned top shell. Tomato concasse is diced, skinless, seedless tomato.

1 oz.	sea asparagus
1 tsp.	tomato concasse
1 tsp.	chopped Maui onion
2 whole	Kona abalone (live, shell on)
$\frac{1}{16}$ tsp.	salt (a pinch)
1 tsp.	kizami wasabi

1. In a small bowl, combine the kizami wasabi, tomato concasse and chopped Maui onion, lightly massage until combined and set aside.
2. Rinse the abalone to remove any debris from the shell or flesh.
3. Place a paring knife just under the flesh next to the shell and dislodge the meat by cutting in a circular motion, clockwise or counter clockwise, to remove the flesh.
4. Quickly cut away the entrails of the abalone and slice the flesh into $\frac{1}{8}$-in. slices.
5. Place half of the sea asparagus into each empty shell to form a bedding and artfully place the sliced abalone meat on top of the sea asparagus bedding in a shingled pattern.
6. Place half of the lomi mixture in the center of each and serve on a bed of crushed ice.

Nutrition Facts

Serving Size (76g)
Servings Per Container

Amount Per Serving

Calories 60   Calories from Fat 0

% Daily Value*

Total Fat 0g	**0%**
Saturated Fat 0g	**0%**
Cholesterol 50mg	**16%**
Sodium 250mg	**11%**
Total Carbohydrate 4g	**1%**
Dietary Fiber 0g	**0%**
Sugars 1g	
Protein 10g	

Grilled Kona Abalone with Hot Miso Sauce

Makes 4 servings   *Alan Tsuchiyama*

As a child, Chef Alan remembers grilling large live 'opihi (limpets) that he snatched off the rocks. This was a great pūpū to eat just before the grass-fed cattle steaks seasoned with Hanapēpē salt went on the grill. Big Island Abalone is a perfect substitute for the scarce, rather difficult-to-get large 'opihi. The Hot Miso Sauce is a recent addition to this 'onolicious pūpū.

½ T.	sake	1 lb.	Big Island Abalone (small to medium)
2 tsp.	mirin	½ T.	shoyu
2 T.	white miso	1 tsp.	sugar
1½ T.	sugar	¼ piece	Hawaiian chili pepper (bird chili) or
½ tsp.	dry hot mustard (Japanese,		Thai chili pepper, minced (amount of
	Chinese or English)		chili pepper may vary depending on
2 tsp.	rice vinegar		your taste)

1. Make the Hot Miso Sauce: In a small saucepan, bring the sake and mirin to a boil. Add the miso and sugar and cook for a minute until the sugar has melted. Stir constantly to keep the miso from burning. Remove from the heat.
2. In a small bowl, slowly add the rice vinegar to the dry hot mustard until a soft paste is formed. Mix until smooth and lump free. Stir the mustard and remaining vinegar into the miso mixture. Reserve the sauce for later.
3. Using a bowl large enough to hold the abalone, rinse the abalone under cold running water. Place abalones shell side down on grill.
4. In a small bowl, mix the shoyu, sugar and chili pepper. Drizzle the shoyu mixture over the grilling abalone.
5. When the abalone begins to boil in its shell, remove from the grill and place a little of the Hot Miso Sauce on top. Serve immediately.

Note: Use disposable gloves when touching chilies or wash your hands well after working with them. The oil from the chilies can remain on your hands for hours and even up to a day. If you rub your eyes, nose or mouth, you might be in for a burn!

Nutrition Facts

Serving Size (148g)
Servings Per Container

Amount Per Serving

Calories 170   Calories from Fat 10

	% Daily Value*
Total Fat 1g	2%
Saturated Fat 0g	0%
Cholesterol 95mg	32%
Sodium 730mg	30%
Total Carbohydrate 18g	6%
Dietary Fiber 2g	7%
Sugars 9g	
Protein 21g	

Simmered Big Island Abalone and Daikon Topped with Scallion and Ginger

Makes 4 servings   *Alan Tsuchiyama*

The Ezo (northern Japan) species of abalone, the one now farmed on the Big Island, is tender and flavorful and loved by many. Chef Alan had the pleasure of eating these as prepared by chef Goro Obara of Maguro-Ya in Kaimukī and even gave his fellow chef a quick lesson in his own recipe. His inspiration led him to create this dish.

4	Big Island abalone, medium size
¾ tsp.	salt
1 small	pot boiling water
2 c.	dashi (bonito stock)
4 slices	daikon (white radish), 1½ inch diameter, ¾ inch thick
1	2-in. piece dashi kombu (dried kelp)
2 T.	mirin
½ c.	sake
1 ½ T.	shoyu
2 T.	vegetable oil
2 T.	minced ginger
2 T.	minced green onion

1. Rinse abalone lightly under cold running water. Rub a teaspoon of salt on each foot (the flesh) of the abalone to clean and remove the natural fluids. Rinse away salt.
2. With the foot positioned up, on the thin edge of the shell, carefully run a clam knife or dinner knife along the shell to release the muscle from the shell. Remove internal organs and mouth.
3. Rinse abalone with water and make diagonal crosshatch incisions about ⅛ inch deep on foot of abalone. Quickly submerge abalone in the boiling water for about one minute. Discard water and rinse abalone with tap water. Reserve the abalone.
4. In a small pot, bring the dashi, daikon and kombu to a simmer for 5 minutes. Add the mirin and sake to the dashi and bring to a simmer.
5. Add the abalone and shoyu and simmer for about 30-45 minutes or until tender.
6. While abalone is simmering, in a very small pot or frying pan, heat the oil until almost smoking, about 375°-400°. Turn off the heat and carefully place the ginger into the hot oil; it might splatter.
7. While the oil is still very hot, add the green onion and ½ tsp. salt, mix and cool to room temperature.
8. Remove the daikon from the dashi and divide into four shallow bowls. Place an abalone on each daikon and pour ¼ c. dashi evenly over each. Top each abalone with the ½ tsp. ginger and scallion (you'll have more than you need).
9. The extra ginger-scallion mixture can be kept in the refrigerator for up to a week and can be used for flavoring your favorite local dishes such as fried rice, fried noodles, poke or stir-fry.

Nutrition Facts

Serving Size (234g)
Servings Per Container

Amount Per Serving

Calories 210   Calories from Fat 80

	% Daily Value*
Total Fat 9g	**14%**
Saturated Fat 1.5g	**7%**
Cholesterol 50mg	**16%**
Sodium 890mg	**37%**
Total Carbohydrate 8g	**3%**
Dietary Fiber 0g	**0%**
Sugars 2g	
Protein 13g	

Kona Kampachi
Yellowtail Amberjack, Kahala

The Kona Kampachi aquaculture operation on the Big Island produces fish that is clean- and crisp-tasting, boasting healthy fats that add richness and heart-healthy properties. You can prepare this versatile fish raw as sashimi or serve it roasted, pan-fried or seared.

Kampachi Ceviche

Makes 3 appetizer servings   *Keoni Chang*

Here's an interesting use for raw kampachi that combines fresh fruit, creamy avocado, crunchy onion, a touch of citrus and the heat of chilies—a veritable symphony in the mouth.

½ lb.	Kona Kampachi or other oily white flesh fish, diced in ¾-in. pieces
3 T.	yuzu juice
⅛ c.	finely sliced Maui onion, rinsed with cold water
1	ruby red grapefruit, segmented and cut into ½-inch dice
1	ripe avocado, diced ¼ inch
½ c.	Hāmākua sweet tomatoes, quartered
3 T.	cilantro, chopped
1	Hawaiian chili pepper, finely minced
1 tsp.	ground Hawaiian salt
	Extra virgin olive oil to taste

1. In a large bowl, combine ingredients except olive oil. Season with Hawaiian salt. Adjust consistency and flavor balance with olive oil.
2. Cover, chill and allow to marinate several hours.
3. Serve in chilled glasses with gaufrette (thin-cut, waffled fresh-fried) potatoes or taro chips.

Nutrition Facts

Serving Size (281g)
Servings Per Container

Amount Per Serving

Calories 220   Calories from Fat 80

	% Daily Value*
Total Fat 9g	**13**%
Saturated Fat 1.5g	**9**%
Cholesterol 35mg	**11**%
Sodium 560mg	**24**%
Total Carbohydrate 17g	**6**%
Dietary Fiber 7g	**27**%
Sugars 9g	
Protein 19g	

Ume Shiso Kampachi on Hawaiian Avocado, Plum Tomato and Crisp Crostini Garnished with Sea Salt

Makes 8 crostinis   *Alan Tsuchiyama*

In this recipe, the flavors of the ingredients are left to speak for themselves. Therefore the freshest products from ocean and land should be used.

8 slices	baguette, sliced ½-inch thick
2 T.	extra virgin olive oil (divided use)
2	vine-ripened plum tomatoes, sliced
½ tsp.	salt
	Fresh-ground black pepper, to taste
½	Hawaiian avocado, peeled and chopped
¼ tsp.	lime juice
4 oz.	Kona Kampachi, blocked for sashimi
1½ tsp.	ume shiso furikake
½ tsp.	sea salt

1. Brush olive oil onto baguette slices. Place on a sheet pan and bake in a 375° oven until light brown and crisp. Remove from oven and cool to room temperature.
2. In a bowl, season sliced tomatoes with salt and pepper and add 2 tsp. olive oil. Mix and place on crostinis.
3. In a bowl, mix the avocado, lime juice, salt and pepper. Place a small mound of avocado on tomato. Season Kona Kampachi block with ume shiso furikake and slice at a slight angle as for sashimi.
4. Place Kona Kampachi on avocado and top with a few grains of sea salt.* Serve.

*If you are lucky enough to receive a gift of Hanapēpē salt from Kaua'i's natural salt pans, we recommend it for this dish, or any very delicate raw or near-cooked dish in which the finishing touch of salt is key. Hanapēpē salt cannot be purchased; it can only be obtained from friends and family of the native Hawaiians permitted to work the pans.

Nutrition Facts

Serving Size (65g)
Servings Per Container

Amount Per Serving

Calories 120   Calories from Fat 50

	% Daily Value*
Total Fat 6g	9%
Saturated Fat 1g	4%
Cholesterol 5mg	2%
Sodium 390mg	16%
Total Carbohydrate 12g	4%
Dietary Fiber 1g	6%
Sugars 1g	
Protein 5g	

Moi
Pacific Threadfin

Moi is famed for having been reserved by early Hawaiians for the ali'i, or royalty—the name is sometimes said to be a play on the word for king or chief (mo'i). The fish were raised in ingenious shoreline ponds with a complex gate system that allowed small fry to swim in and out but trapped their elders once they reached a certain size. In modern times, moi can be found on and around the reefs, but not in great numbers. Aquaculture has brought them back. Buy moi whole (they average 1.5-2 lbs. each) and have the fishmonger dress the fish and save the head and bones to make the broth. Hawai'i farm-raised moi provide a source of EPA and DHA omega-3 fatty acids.

Moi with Fennel

Makes 4 servings   *Dr. Stephen Bradley*

In this classic south-of-France approach, fish fillets are baked in their own juices—a fumet (foo-may) or stock made with the bones and head—on a bed of crunchy, anise-flavored fennel.

For the fish fumet:

	Heads and bones of the filleted moi
1	carrot, chopped
1	onion, chopped
4	peppercorns
2	bay leaves

For the fish:

½ c.	extra virgin olive oil
1	fresh fennel (anise) bulb, finely chopped
2 lbs.	moi, filleted
1 bunch	flat-leaf parsley, chopped
¼ tsp.	sea salt
	Freshly ground black pepper, to taste
¼ c.	fish fumet (fish broth)

1. Make the fumet: Place ingredients in a saucepan, cover with water and gently boil for 15 minutes. Strain and set aside.
2. Prepare the fish: Preheat the oven to 450°. In an oven-proof dish, combine olive oil and fennel.
3. Arrange the moi fillets in the dish and scatter with parsley.
4. Pour in the fish fumet. Place, uncovered, in the oven and cook 10 minutes. Serve immediately.

Nutrition Facts

Serving Size (379g)
Servings Per Container

Amount Per Serving

Calories 580   Calories from Fat 270

	% Daily Value*
Total Fat 31g	47%
Saturated Fat 4g	20%
Cholesterol 105mg	36%
Sodium 310mg	13%
Total Carbohydrate 9g	3%
Dietary Fiber 3g	12%
Sugars 2g	
Protein 60g	

Bundle of Moi

Makes 4 servings   *Wanda A. Adams*

Here's an unusual technique: Fish, in this case fillets of moi, is encased in foil bundles with vegetables and seasonings and "baked" in a covered pan on the stove top. Cooking takes just minutes and the juices are contained—perfect for drizzling over hot rice. Although many people use foil only for the bundles, some object to prolonged contact between food and foil, especially if there's acid in the recipe; it can create off flavors. The answer is to line the foil with kitchen parchment. For the bundles, you will need kitchen parchment and aluminum foil in four 12-inch-square pieces. You'll also need a roomy, heavy-bottomed frying pan or Dutch oven with a lid. A well-seasoned cast iron frying pan would be perfect as well.

	Vegetable oil or oil spray
4 pieces	moi fillet (4 oz. each)
	Freshly ground pepper, to taste
8	shrimp, peeled and deveined
1 c.	shelled edamame
½ c.	carrots, peeled and cut into 2-inch length matchsticks
¼ c.	shallots or sweet onions, minced
4 T.	sake
2 T.	shoyu

1. For each bundle, lay a square of aluminum foil on the counter and top with square of kitchen parchment. Brush parchment very lightly with oil or spray with cooking spray.
2. Season both sides of a fillet of moi with salt and pepper and place in center of bundle. Place 2 shrimp on top of moi fillet. Scatter one quarter of vegetables over and around fish.
3. In a bowl, whisk together sake and shoyu.
4. Draw up sides of bundle and drizzle ¼ of the sake-soy mixture over the fish and vegetables. Fold left and right sides of parchment one over the other, then draw up top and bottom and fold over and over to make a bundle. Fold and crimp foil around parchment packet in the same manner. Repeat with remaining ingredients.

Nutrition Facts

Serving Size (208g)
Servings Per Container

Amount Per Serving

Calories 240   Calories from Fat 25

	% Daily Value*
Total Fat 3g	4%
Saturated Fat 0g	0%
Cholesterol 75mg	25%
Sodium 270mg	11%
Total Carbohydrate 9g	3%
Dietary Fiber 3g	10%
Sugars 2g	
Protein 37g	

5. Place skillet or Dutch oven on burner, bring to medium heat. To prevent burning or sticking, spray with oil spray or pour in no more than ¼ inch of water.

6. Place packets in pan, cover and bake about 10 minutes. Remove from heat and allow packets to steam in their own juices a few minutes more.

7. To serve, use a spatula to lift moi and shrimp onto a bed of hot rice or other grains, scatter with vegetables and drizzle juices over.

Minute Poke

Makes 1 serving   *Alan Wong*

Chef-restaurateur Alan Wong sent in a moi dish with these notes: "Minute Poke is a name I made up. It's a poke dish designed for the diner to mix at the table, so it marinates briefly just before it's eaten. 'Miko' is the Hawaiian word for 'to season or salt,' but in casual usage it means 'to let sit for a while.' Poke can be eaten fresh or prepared ahead of time."

5 oz.	moi, thinly sliced
3 T.	green onion, thinly sliced
⅓ c.	round onion, small-diced
1½ tsp.	sambal oelek (Indonesian chili sauce)
1 t.	oyster sauce
1 t.	shoyu
1½ tsp.	'inamona (ground or finely chopped roasted kukui nut relish)
¼ tsp.	minced ginger
	Various fresh seaweeds, for garnish
⅛ tsp.	Hawaiian salt, for garnish

1. Cut the moi into thin slices. Place in a small mixing bowl. Cover and refrigerate until needed.
2. Thinly slice the green onion and small-dice the round onion. Each ingredient should be stored individually in small ramekins or mixing bowls, covered and refrigerated.
3. In a small bowl, combine the sambal oelek, oyster sauce, shoyu, sesame oil, 'inamona and minced ginger. Mix well and set aside.
4. Place a rectangular musubi mold (1¾ in. by 3½ in. by 2½ in.) in the middle of a shallow serving bowl.
5. Layer the poke ingredients in the mold in the following order: fish, diced round onions, thinly sliced moi, green onions. Press down and unmold. Refrigerate until ready to serve.
6. Before serving, spoon the poke sauce around the musubi-shaped poke, or serve the sauce on the side.
7. Garnish with a small pile of Hawaiian salt and arrange the seaweeds around the rim of the bowl.
8. The diner mixes the sauce, salt and seaweed with the poke to taste, creating an individual traditional poke in less than a minute, hence the name "Minute Poke."

Nutrition Facts	
Serving Size (272g)	
Servings Per Container	
Amount Per Serving	
Calories 270	Calories from Fat 35
	% Daily Value*
Total Fat 4g	6%
Saturated Fat 0g	0%
Cholesterol 65mg	22%
Sodium 630mg	26%
Total Carbohydrate 16g	5%
Dietary Fiber 4g	15%
Sugars 7g	
Protein 40g	

The Simplest Moi Recipe Ever

Makes 3-4 servings   *Wanda A. Adams*

Don't overcomplicate with a delicious fish. This technique has been used in Hawai'i for generations, with cooks adding an ingredient or two—a splash of shoyu, a squeeze of lemon, a drizzle of vinegar. But basically, it's salt, fish and the slightly vegetal smoky scent of ti leaf.

8-10	ti leaves, washed, thick ribs removed or shaved down
1 tsp.	Hawaiian salt (white, alae'a or black)
1 whole	moi (1½ -2 lbs.)
	Additional flavoring, if desired

1. Clean and dress moi or have the fishmonger do so.
2. Preheat oven to 350°. In a large, flat oiled roasting pan, lay out 4-5 ti leaves horizontally and on top of these, 4-5 vertically.
3. Place the moi on top of ti leaves and salt the fish on both sides with a somewhat generous hand.
4. Drizzle on both sides with whatever you like—sesame oil to hot sauce (optional).
5. Wrap ti leaf ends around fish, tucking in. Bake for 20-25 minutes to an internal temperature (use instant-read thermometer) of 135° F at thickest part.

Nutrition Facts

Serving Size (266g)
Servings Per Container

Amount Per Serving

Calories 340   Calories from Fat 25

% Daily Value*

Total Fat 2.5g	**4%**
Saturated Fat 0g	**0%**
Cholesterol 125mg	**41%**
Sodium 680mg	**28%**
Total Carbohydrate 0g	**0%**
Dietary Fiber 0g	**0%**
Sugars 0g	
Protein 69g	

Tilapia
Sun Fish

Commercial tilapia growing is on the rise in Hawai'i, as the fish gains popularity among high-end restaurants. Island farm-raised tilapia is clean, fresh and mild-flavored, and versatile enough to allow many different preparation methods. Farm-raised freshwater tilapia are a different species than those swimming in the Ala Wai Canal, and they live in a vastly different environment, in which water quality and food sources are carefully managed. U.S. tilapia operations get the thumbs-up from the tough Seafood Watch evaluators at the Monterey Bay Aquarium. Tilapia, which thrives in warm waters, is soft textured and lean. It's an extremely versatile fish for almost any cooking method—from steaming to sautéeing to frying. Although not as rich in EPA and DHA as many other seafood options, farmed tilapia is a good source of protein, selenium and vitamins B_3 and B_6.

Fish Jun Fritatta

Makes 2 servings   *Sharon Kobayashi*

This tilapia fritatta cooks in 5 minutes, satisfying a craving for Korean take-out quickly, economically and with less salt and fat. Pickled ginger has a clean, bright flavor, complementing the fish perfectly.

4 oz.	tilapia fillet, fresh (substitute frozen, defrosted)
2 tsp.	teriyaki sauce
½ tsp.	sriracha hot sauce (or to taste)
½ tsp.	sesame seed oil
½ tsp.	cornstarch
½ tsp.	shoyu
¼ c.	egg substitute*
2 each	egg, large, beaten
⅓ c.	garlic chives, minced (nira)
½ tsp.	vegetable oil
2 tsp.	pickled ginger, shredded (or substitute kim chee)

1. Marinate fish in teriyaki sauce, sriracha, sesame oil and cornstarch for 20 minutes.
2. Bring the fish to room temperature and pre-heat the broiler.
3. Pre-heat a small non-stick or cast iron skillet (make sure it can safely go under the broiler) on medium heat.
4. Combine soy sauce, egg substitute, eggs and chives. Add the oil to the skillet, swirling to coat. Add egg mixture, allow to set briefly.
5. Place fish in the center of the egg, allowing some of the egg mixture to run over the edges of the fish. Pour any marinating juices over the top of the fish, and cook for 3 minutes.
6. Transfer the pan to the broiler for 2 minutes or till the top is golden brown. Sprinkle with ginger. Serve hot or at room temperature.

* Use vegan dried products, made from seeds and other vegetable materials, or the liquid variety made from egg whites found in the chill case of most grocery stores.

Nutrition Facts

Serving Size (163g)
Servings Per Container

Amount Per Serving

Calories 190   Calories from Fat 80

	% Daily Value*
Total Fat 9g	**14**%
Saturated Fat 2.5g	**12**%
Cholesterol 240mg	**80**%
Sodium 600mg	**25**%
Total Carbohydrate 3g	**1**%
Dietary Fiber less than 1g	**2**%
Sugars 2g	
Protein 22g	

Crispy Baked Tilapia and Creole Vegetables

Makes 4 servings   *Sharon Kobayashi*

This is a great recipe for kids, with complex flavors and textures and relatively little knife-work required. It is easy to cut this recipe in half; just use an 8- to 9-in.-square pan.

1 lb.	tilapia fillet (four 4-oz. fillets)	1 c.	okra, diced (fresh or frozen)
2 T.	Worcestershire sauce, divided use	¼ tsp.	cayenne pepper (or to taste)
4 T.	flour	½ c.	marinara sauce
2 T.	reduced-fat mayonnaise	4 T.	salsa
1 c.	cornflakes, crushed	4 T.	white wine
2 stalks	celery, diced	⅔ c.	reduced-sodium chicken broth
1	bell pepper, diced	2 T.	unsalted butter
1 c.	frozen vegetables, southwest blend (such as C&W brand)	1 tsp.	dried thyme

1. Preheat oven to 375° F. Rub the fillets with 1 teaspoon of Worcestershire sauce and dredge both sides in flour. Spread the mayonnaise evenly on 1 side of each fillet (use your fingers).
2. Dredge the mayonnaise-coated side in cornflakes (pressing down to get good coverage) and set aside. Spray a 9-by-13-in. pan with cooking spray, or use a non-stick baking dish.
3. Add celery, bell pepper, frozen vegetables, okra, cayenne, marinara, salsa, wine, broth and remaining teaspoon Worcestershire sauce. Dot the top with butter.
4. Lay fillets over vegetables (cornflake side up), and sprinkle thyme over all. Carefully transfer casserole to the oven (hold steady to keep liquid from splashing over the fish).
5. Bake for 35-40 minutes or till pan juices are reduced and thickened. Serve immediately.

Nutrition Facts

Serving Size (359g)
Servings Per Container

Amount Per Serving

Calories 300   Calories from Fat 80

	% Daily Value*
Total Fat 9g	**14**%
Saturated Fat 4.5g	**23**%
Cholesterol 70mg	**24**%
Sodium 500mg	**21**%
Total Carbohydrate 27g	**9**%
Dietary Fiber 4g	**17**%
Sugars 6g	
Protein 27g	

Sunshine Citrus Tilapia

Makes 4 servings   *Carol Nardello*

Here oranges and lemons perk up the flavor of the fish. Serve on a bed of coconut rice (jasmine rice sauteed briefly in a little butter, then steamed in half coconut milk, half water).

2 T.	flour
⅛ tsp.	salt
⅛ tsp.	white pepper
1 lb.	tilapia fillets
1 T.	butter
1 T.	oil
1 each	Kā'ū orange, juiced
	Zest and juice of 1 small Meyer lemon
1 tsp.	grated fresh ginger

1. In a shallow bowl, combine the flour, salt and pepper. Lightly dredge the fillets in the seasoned flour.
2. In a large skillet over medium heat, add the oil and butter. When the butter has melted, add the fish and cook for about 2 minutes per side, or until golden and just cooked through.
3. Remove the fish from the pan and set aside. Add the orange juice, lemon zest and lemon juice with the ginger. Decrease the heat to low and simmer for 2 minutes or until thickened, stirring occasionally. Taste and adjust seasonings.
4. Return the fish to the skillet, baste with sauce and cook for 2 minutes or until heated through. Avoid overcooking.

Nutrition Facts

Serving Size (174g)
Servings Per Container

Amount Per Serving

Calories 200   Calories from Fat 80

	% Daily Value*
Total Fat 8g	13%
Saturated Fat 3g	14%
Cholesterol 65mg	21%
Sodium 150mg	6%
Total Carbohydrate 8g	3%
Dietary Fiber 1g	6%
Sugars 2g	
Protein 24g	

Parmesan- and Almond-Encrusted Tilapia

Makes 4 servings   *Carol Nardello*

This is the sort of recipe you can throw together after work, using tilapia or whatever white-meat fish fillets you pick up on the way home.

½ c.	sliced almonds
½ c.	panko (Japanese breadcrumbs)
3 T.	freshly grated Parmesan cheese
1 tsp.	garlic powder
2 tsp.	salt-free lemon pepper seasoning
½ tsp.	paprika
1 lb.	tilapia fillets (or comparable fish)
2 T.	olive oil

1. Preheat oven to 400° F.
2. In a bowl, combine almonds, panko, cheese and seasonings. Brush fish lightly with oil.
3. Coat fish evenly with crumb mixture. Place fish on a greased or oil-sprayed sheet tray.
4. Bake in hot oven for 8 to 10 minutes or until desired doneness.

Nutrition Facts

Serving Size (145g)
Servings Per Container

Amount Per Serving

Calories 290   Calories from Fat 140

	% Daily Value*
Total Fat 16g	**25**%
Saturated Fat 3g	**14**%
Cholesterol 60mg	**20**%
Sodium 360mg	**15**%
Total Carbohydrate 9g	**3**%
Dietary Fiber 2g	**7**%
Sugars 1g	
Protein 28g	

Quick and Lively Fish Soup

Makes 4 servings   *Carol Nardello*

There's nothing like a bowl of hot soup on a chilly day and a little spice to add to the heat. And if it's easy to make, too, that's a bonus.

2 T.	olive oil
1	onion, chopped
½	yellow bell pepper, diced
½	red bell pepper, diced
2 cloves	garlic, minced
2 tsp.	chili powder
1 tsp.	ground cumin
¼ tsp.	cayenne pepper (optional)
1 can	Ro-Tel tomatoes with chilies* (10 oz.)
1 can	fire-roasted diced tomatoes (14.5 oz.)
4 oz.	fish or clam broth
4 oz.	water
1 lb.	tilapia, diced in ½-inch cubes
½	lime, cut in wedges
5 T.	cilantro, chopped

1. Heat a large soup pot on medium heat. Add oil and onions. Sauté for 5 minutes.
2. Add peppers and garlic. Sauté 1-2 minutes. Stir in chili powder, cumin and cayenne.
3. Add both cans of tomatoes with broth and water. Stir well. Bring to a boil. Reduce heat to low and simmer covered for 10 minutes.
4. Stir in fish and simmer 3-5 minutes more or just until cooked through. Garnish with a squeeze of lime juice and a sprinkle of cilantro.

Ro-Tel tomatoes are a brand of tomatoes canned with diced green chilies of various kinds. If you can't find them, substitute with a second can of the fire-roasted diced tomatoes, plus a 4-oz. can of diced green chilies.

Nutrition Facts

Serving Size (436g)
Servings Per Container

Amount Per Serving

Calories 250   Calories from Fat 90

	% Daily Value*
Total Fat 10g	**15%**
Saturated Fat 2g	**9%**
Cholesterol 55mg	**19%**
Sodium 680mg	**29%**
Total Carbohydrate 15g	**5%**
Dietary Fiber 4g	**18%**
Sugars 6g	
Protein 26g	

'Ono Orzo and Fish Pasta

Makes 6-8 servings   *Carol Nardello*

This is a hearty fish casserole-type of dish which is never overcooked. The fish is cooked in the sauce and stirred into prepared pasta and garnished with fresh basil and grated cheese. So quick and delicious!

2 T.	olive oil	½ tsp.	sugar
1 c.	onion, chopped	½ tsp.	salt
3 cloves	garlic, minced	2 lbs.	tilapia or other mild, flaky fish, lightly
¼ tsp.	red pepper flakes		seasoned with salt and pepper
1 tsp.	Italian seasoning	1 lb.	orzo pasta, cooked and drained
⅓ c.	white wine	3 T.	Italian parsley, chopped
1	lemon, zested and juiced	½ c.	Parmesan cheese, grated
1 can	diced tomatoes (15 oz.)	1 handful	fresh basil leaves, thinly sliced

1. Prepare pasta according to package directions. Keep warm.
2. Pre-heat a large skillet on medium heat.
3. Add oil and onions. Sauté for 3-4 minutes. Add garlic, red pepper flakes and Italian seasoning, stirring well.
4. Add wine, lemon zest and juice, tomatoes, sugar and salt. Bring to a boil. Reduce heat and add seasoned fish to pan.
5. Submerge fish in sauce and cover tightly. Simmer for 10-15 minutes or until desired doneness. Avoid overcooking.
6. Stir Italian parsley and fish with sauce into pasta and toss gently.
7. Pour into serving bowl and top with cheese and fresh basil.

Nutrition Facts

Serving Size (364g)
Servings Per Container

Amount Per Serving

Calories 530   Calories from Fat 90

	% Daily Value*
Total Fat 10g	**16**%
Saturated Fat 3g	**15**%
Cholesterol 80mg	**27**%
Sodium 480mg	**20**%
Total Carbohydrate 65g	**22**%
Dietary Fiber 4g	**17**%
Sugars 7g	
Protein 44g	

Sautéed Lemongrass Tilapia with Coconut-Curried Sweet Potato Puree

Makes 6-8 servings   *Alan Tsuchiyama*

Chef Alan was skeptical about farm-raised tilapia at first, but he is a believer now. This is a sustainable fish that can be raised in either fresh or salt water. The tilapia is recognized for its beautiful white, moist and flaky flesh with a mild clean flavor, which makes it a very versatile fish to cook with.

2 stalks	lemongrass, white to light green, chopped	1 T.	sesame oil
4 leaves	Thai basil	4 fillets	tilapia, skinned with bones removed
¼ cup	round onion, chopped	1 lb.	sweet potato, peeled, cut into large chunks
2 cloves	garlic, chopped	¾ c.	coconut milk
1	Thai chili, chopped	1 T.	Thai curry paste, your choice of flavor (green, yellow, red or penang)
1 T.	sugar		Flour as needed for dredging
1 T.	lime juice		Canola oil for frying
1 T.	shoyu		
2 tsp.	fish sauce		

1. Place the lemongrass in a blender or mini food processor with Thai basil, onion, garlic, Thai chili, sugar, lime juice, shoyu, fish sauce and sesame oil and blend to a puree.
2. In a flat dish, marinate the tilapia with the lemongrass puree for about 30 minutes. In a steamer or pot of water, cook the sweet potato until soft. Place sweet potato in a mixing bowl. In a saucepan, bring coconut milk and Thai curry paste to a boil and add it to the sweet potato; mix with a wire whisk to puree. Keep sweet potato puree warm (place it in a heat-proof covered bowl in a pot of hot water).
3. Remove tilapia from marinade and drain off excess liquid. Lightly dust the tilapia with the flour. In a skillet, heat canola oil and fry tilapia until done. It will take only a few minutes per side. Serve tilapia with sweet potato.

Nutrition Facts

Serving Size (316g)
Servings Per Container

Amount Per Serving

Calories 350   Calories from Fat 130

% Daily Value*

Total Fat 15g	**22%**
Saturated Fat 9g	**46%**
Cholesterol 55mg	**19%**
Sodium 720mg	**30%**
Total Carbohydrate 31g	**10%**
Dietary Fiber 4g	**17%**
Sugars 9g	
Protein 26g	

Miso-Poached Tilapia with Udon Noodles

Makes 4 servings

Carol Nardello

Hearty udon (buckwheat noodles) and delicate fish (tilapia, monchong or mahimahi) is an intriguing combination in this recipe, whose sauce makes use of brightly flavored red miso (soy bean paste). Admittedly, the sodium count of miso is a bit high, but here, a small bit extends its influence to four servings, perfect for a chilly evening.

4 c.	chicken broth, low sodium
2 T.	miso paste
1 c.	white wine or sake
3 oz.	shiitake mushrooms, sliced
4 stalks	green onions, sliced
2 tsp.	shoyu, low sodium
1 lb.	tilapia fillets*
12 oz.	udon noodles

1. Bring a large pot of water to a boil.
2. In a large skillet over medium heat, combine broth, miso, wine, mushrooms, half of the green onion slices and the shoyu. Whisk to blend well and dissolve miso.
3. Reduce heat to low and add the fish fillets.
4. Cover tightly and poach gently for 8 to 10 minutes or to desired doneness.
5. Cook udon noodles in the pot of boiling water according to package directions.
6. Drain well and divide among 4 large bowls.
7. Add broth with vegetables and top with poached fish.
8. Garnish with reserved green onion slices.

* Tilapia fillets work well, but you can also substitute monchong or mahimahi fillets.

Nutrition Facts

Serving Size (543g)
Servings Per Container

Amount Per Serving

Calories 300   Calories from Fat 40

	% Daily Value*
Total Fat 4.5g	**7%**
Saturated Fat 1g	**6%**
Cholesterol 55mg	**19%**
Sodium 770mg	**32%**
Total Carbohydrate 26g	**9%**
Dietary Fiber 1g	**5%**
Sugars 2g	
Protein 32g	

Contributors

Wanda A. Adams, *co-editor*
Wanda Adams is a Honolulu writer and editor with 30-plus years' experience writing about food. She is the author of four cookbooks, editor of two. Her specialty is the history of local-style recipes. www.ourislandplate.com

Stephen Bradley, *contributor and essayist*
Dr. Stephen Bradley, MD, is the medical director of and practices adult/preventive medicine and bariatric medicine at the Wai'anae Coast Comprehensive Health Center and is a board member of the American Heart Association, Hawai'i Division. Dr. Bradley is also a chef, trained in Bologna, Italy, and a graduate of the California Culinary Academy in San Francisco.

Adriana Torres Chong, *contributor, food stylist and photographer*
Adriana Torres-Chong holds a bachelor's degree in gastronomy from the Universidad del Claustro de Sor Juana in Mexico City. Her food styling and photography work can be found in national and international publications. *A Splash of Aloha* is her eighth cookbook. She has taught courses in Mexican cuisine at Kapi'olani Community College since 2007. www.adriana-torreschong.com

Kusuma Cooray, *contributor*
Kusuma Cooray, CEC, CCE, CHE, FCFA (CG), trained at Le Cordon Bleu, the National Baking School (London) and La Varenne Ecole de Cuisine (Paris). She was executive chef at the renowned Honolulu restaurant The Willows and at The Banyan Gardens. Chef Cooray is currently a professor and chef instructor at the Culinary Institute of the Pacific at Kapi'olani Community College.

Magdy El-Zoheiry, *contributor*

A native of Alexandria, Egypt, Chef Magdy El-Zoheiry moved to Hawai'i in 1992, where he helped open the Middle Eastern restaurants Hajibaba and The Pyramids. After graduating from KCC in 1999, he worked at French, Italian and American restaurants in Honolulu, Las Vegas and New York City. Since 2005, Chef Magdy has been teaching Middle Eastern cuisines as a featured chef instructor in KCC's continuing education culinary program.

Eddie Fernandez, *contributor*

A native of Kaua'i and a graduate of Kapi'olani Community College, Chef Eddie Fernandez rose from prep cook to corporate executive chef for the Nick's Fishmarket chain in 27 years with that company. In 1988 he was opening executive chef for the legendary Black Orchid restaurant and later moved on to Nickolas Nicholas. In 1991, he joined his alma mater as a chef-instructor.

Frank Gonzales, *co-editor*

Frank Gonzales is program manager for the Continuing Education Culinary Arts Program at Kapi'olani Community College. His responsibilities include designing and implementing public and contract culinary education and training programs. Frank is a graduate of Stanford University and holds a bachelor's degree in international relations. He is also an alumnus of KCC and holds Associate of Science degrees in culinary arts and patisserie.

Henry Holthaus, *contributor and essayist*

Chef Henry Holthaus has been a chef instructor in the culinary arts department at Kapi'olani Community College since 1992. He is a nationally recognized expert on food safety and has served as an editor for the National Restaurant Association Educational Foundation's ServSafe certification exam. Chef Henry is a certified ServSafe food safety instructor at KCC. His television show on food safety— *Shig Happens!*—airs on Olelo 55 in Hawai'i.

Scott Iwamura, *recipe analyst*

Scott Iwamura is a senior in the dietetics program at the University of Hawai'i-Mānoa. A research assistant under book contributor Dr. Corilee Watters, he conducted the nutrient analysis of the book's recipes. He aspires to become a clinical registered dietitian and plans to pursue a graduate degree in nutritional science. He strongly believes that proper nutrition is the cornerstone to good health and that it is never too late to adopt healthy dietary habits.

Sharon Kobayashi, *contributor*

Entrepreneur and chef Sharon Kobayashi, formerly a biologist, elected mid-career to earn a culinary arts degree from the Culinary Institute of the Pacific at Kapi'olani Community College. Her restaurant experiences have taken her from Hawai'i to Washington to California and include French, Pacific Rim, Japanese fusion, vegan and raw food creations. She is the founder of Akamai Foods and was a co-author of *A DASH of Aloha* (2007) and A *Sweet Dash of Aloha* (2011). www.akamaifoods.com

Daniel Leung, *project coordinator and co-editor*

Daniel Leung holds a master's degree in social work from the University of Hawai'i and an associate's degree in culinary arts from Kapi'olani Community College. He is a program coordinator at the Culinary Institute of the Pacific at KCC. His responsibilities include developing and implementing applied nutrition and culinary education programs. He is also a continuing education culinary instructor.

George Mavrothalassitis, *contributor*

A past winner of the James Beard Award, George Mavrothalassitis is chef-proprietor of Honolulu's top-rated Chef Mavro restaurant. He is a founding member of Hawai'i Regional Cuisine, and his restaurant is the only Island restaurant to earn the American Automobile Association's Five-Diamond Award.

Carol Nardello, *contributor*

Carol Nardello is a chef-instructor with the continuing education program at the Culinary Institute of the Pacific at KCC. Previously, she worked for seven years as executive chef for the Sub-Zero/Wolf Honolulu showroom. Chef Carol specializes in gluten-free foods, easy entertaining, healthy cooking and nutrition for families and has been a specialist trainer for after-school programs educating children about good nutrition.

Grant Sato, *contributor*

Grant Sato is purchasing manager and chef-instructor with the continuing education culinary arts program at KCC. Born, raised and educated in the Islands, he combines his award-winning teaching techniques (2001 Francis Davis Award for Outstanding Undergraduate Teaching, University of Hawai'i System) with culinary skills honed in Asia and at local hotels and restaurants.

Karl Sloss, *contributor*

Karl Sloss is a dietetics student at the University of Hawai'i-Mānoa working as a research assistant to Dr. Corilee Watters on projects involving local aquaculture, fatty acid composition of seafood and science curriculum for school gardens. An athlete who went to undergraduate school on a tennis scholarship, he has a bachelor's degree in psychology. Karl also studied culinary arts at Johnson & Wales University before returning to Hawai'i to study nutrition.

Ronald Takahashi, *principal investigator and co-editor*

Ronald Takahashi is a professor and department chair at the Culinary Institute of the Pacific at Kapi'olani Community College. He has more than 40 years of professional and academic experience in the food and beverage industry. During his academic career, he has taught courses in hospitality purchasing and cost control, dining room service, food service supervision, menu merchandising, equipment layout and design, and the hospitality industry.

Kevin Tate, *contributor*

A self-taught cook and entrepreneur, Kevin Tate owned and operated the much-loved Kailua Southern food/Italian cuisine restaurant Kevin's Two Boots. He continues to cater, work as a private chef and teach classes at KCC's continuing education culinary arts program.

Alan Tsuchiyama, *contributor*

Chef Alan Tsuchiyama is an associate professor of culinary arts at the Culinary Institute of the Pacific at Kapiʻolani Community College. He is a KCC graduate and worked at the Kāhala Hilton Hotel and the Drake and Fairmont Hotels in Chicago before returning to Hawaiʻi to become executive sous chef for the Sheraton Waikīkī. In 1999 Chef Alan joined the instructional staff at KCC, where he has specialized in preparing students for culinary competitions.

Corilee Watters, *contributor and essayist*

Dr. Corilee Watters is an assistant professor of nutrition at the University of Hawaiʻi-Mānoa in the Department of Human Nutrition, Food and Animal Science. She has a doctorate in nutrition and metabolism from the University of Alberta and a master of science in nutrition from the University of Aberdeen in Great Britain. Corilee is a registered dietitian who also worked as a cardiology dietitian and a coordinator of nutrition services in health care.

Alan Wong, *contributor*

Chef-restaurateur Alan Wong is a James Beard Award winner (1996) and an alumnus of the culinary arts program at KCC and the Culinary Institute of America. After working at the Greenbriar in West Virginia, Lutece in New York and the Canoe House on the Big Island, he opened Alan Wong's Restaurant in 1995 and Alan Wong's Pineapple Room in 1999.

Index of Recipes